WHY
MARIANNE
FAITHFULL
MATTERS

WHY

MARIANNE

FAITHFULL

MATTERS

TANYA PEARSON

faber

First published in the UK in 2021
by Faber & Faber Ltd
Bloomsbury House
74–77 Great Russell Street
London WC1B 3DA

First published in the USA in 2021
by University of Texas Press
P.O. Box 7819
Austin, TX 78713-7819

Printed and bound by CPI Group (UK) Ltd, Croydon, CR0 4YY

A CIP record for this book
is available from the British library

ISBN 978–0–571–36896–9

For Marianne Faithfull

CONTENTS

INTRODUCTION: WOMEN ARE BORN CULTURAL ARCHAEOLOGISTS

Women are born cultural archaeologists, forced to mine for evidence of our histories in a vast expanse of male-dominated and male-curated media. I am a punk and a hustler at heart, but as I've aged and stumbled into the academic world by way of oral history, I've become aware of historical gender discrepancies and the seeming deliberateness with which certain voices—black voices, brown voices, queer voices, indigenous voices—are muzzled and made illegible in rock history and scholarship. While racism and homophobia continue to silence these voices, the subject of this book is a white, heterosexual woman from London. No matter how arbitrary it may seem, especially in this post-gender age, gender continues to be used as a tool to build a revisionist history that excludes women. It has been weaponized to validate the masculine and invalidate the feminine. Rock history falls into the same trap as other histories, placing emphasis on "valid," quantifiable historical evidence and dismissing memory, memoir, biography, and experiential history as both frivolous and dangerous to the canon. Memory is the Yoko Ono of scholarship.

As a closeted teenage homosexual, I spent a lot of time alone in my room, avoiding high school boys and their aggressive penises, playing music, drawing, adventuring in a homemade spy belt, and recording music videos and live performances on VHS tape—before the dawn of the internet and when MTV still lived up to its name. I collected rock music encyclopedias, memoirs, and autobiographies. When I managed to get a ride to the mall, I visited the bookstore first and ordered obscure music books about female artists to the frustration of the geriatric staff. My family acquired AOL dial-up internet when I was seventeen, which facilitated my obsessive detective work. I did not know who Marianne Faithfull was until November 6, 1997, when I saw her perform on *Saturday Night Live* with Metallica. I recognized her image, of course, since her legacy is often relegated to the confines of the 60s blonde bombshell, but I hadn't been properly introduced to the history behind that image, and I'm still resentful about it. Metallica performed "The Memory Remains," the first single from the album *Reload*. I wasn't a huge fan of Metallica—I associated them with my hypermasculine, cockrocking high school peers—but I was drawn to the beautiful older woman in a black suit, stage left, who periodically "la la'ed" into her microphone. She was enigmatic, seemed important, and had great hair. Consequently, *Reload* was the first Metallica album I ever purchased.

Marianne Faithfull rose to fame, accidentally, during the dawn of the media age in 1960s London, on the arm of Mick Jagger. However short-lived the relationship, it has become a defining characteristic of her image and her legacy. She has been a lot of things: a virgin, a celebrity, a model, a singer, an actress, a mother, a groupie, a girlfriend, a wife, a whore, and an addict. But, unlike other women who were attached to prominent men and vilified in the press (ahem, Yoko, Courtney), Marianne engineered a successful comeback *and* she did so out of the rubble of heroin addiction and abject humiliation. Her addiction helped extricate her from pop stardom and the shadow of the Rolling Stones. She has released music consistently, I would argue prolifically, since 1979, reinventing herself as a serious artist and chanteuse. Hers is a story of redemption not often granted to women in the industry.

This redemption is not easy to pinpoint, though, because it cannot be narrowed down to a single moment. Some would argue that *Broken English* was it, but she hadn't yet achieved sobriety. I would argue her redemption is more complicated than any single moment, that in truth, it is a series of personal events and releases culminating in an ever-expanding catalogue of interesting work and a personal history unparalleled in rock music.

Faithfull's good looks were the catalyst that launched her career. She was one of the first female singers to make a mark during the British Invasion with hits like "As Tears Go By," "Yesterday," "Come and Stay with Me," and "It's

All Over Now, Baby Blue." She was a celebrity before she was a bona fide artist, and her relationship with Jagger, unapologetic sexual exploits, and drug use made her a polarizing figure at the end of the 1960s when Cold War propaganda and anti-communist sentiment acted as an antidote to the freedoms purported by Swinging Sixties culture. She spent much of the 1970s battling heroin addiction and the mythology that had grown around her and reemerged in 1979 with *Broken English*, a cult classic and her official comeback. She released consecutive albums in the 1980s, experimenting with different styles and genres, effectively distancing herself from the singular 1960s folk/pop princess image, and reinventing herself as a torch singer with substance and depth. In the 1990s and 2000s, collaborations with a younger generation of rock royalty—Nick Cave, Warren Ellis, PJ Harvey, Cat Power, Beck, Anna Calvi, and Mark Lanegan, among others—proved both her relevancy as an artist and her indisputable gifts as a songwriter and collaborator. *Negative Capability*, released in November 2018, is her most personal album to date, dealing with themes of love, loss, loneliness, and terrorism. She remains attuned to contemporary culture, more than fifty years after she entered the music industry, a feat not often accomplished by women in their mid-seventies.

I got into Marianne Faithfull much too late, but once I found her, I fell in love. I am an addict through and through and so I am a glutton for pleasure. Marianne Faithfull's music is a pleasure, and I want to write about that. She has been the soundtrack for much of my sober, out and proud adult life; her life, lyrics, and artistry a blueprint for living fearlessly and authentically. As an academic, I feel a duty to remain cold, distant, and objective. To unnecessarily complicate simple facts or experiential truths. But I am a fan above all else, and so my interest in Marianne Faithfull's astrological signs and planetary placements is scholarly by proxy. I want to write what I genuinely care about with the confidence of a mediocre white man, but armed with the knowledge to back up my convictions, with a genuine self-awareness, and, hopefully, with none of the self-delusion.

In 1995, Faithfull recorded *A Secret Life*, a rock album that incorporated classical and blues music. She collaborated with *Twin Peaks* composer Angelo Badalamenti, who, from working with David Lynch, had developed a particular approach. According to Marianne, he insisted on "Fragments, fragments, fragments!" while she preferred to shape and refine a whole song or story over time.[1] In true Badalamenti fashion, I have compiled a book of fragments, detailing the most pertinent aspects of Marianne Faithfull's life and career, for people who love her and for people who are interested in getting to know her.

One of my main goals in life is to create a kind of feminist media empire to disseminate information about women-identified rock musicians across various media platforms. I think the most powerful thing we (the collective we) can do as music lovers is to talk about the musicians we love, to saturate popular culture, and to flesh out the rock narrative. This is especially important for women, for queers, for people of color, many of whom have heroically taken it upon themselves to document their own histories and to build a cultural context that represents them.

My biggest complaint about mainstream popular music media is that it tends to venerate traditional rock icons and focus on what's new at the expense of building a more diverse knowledge base in the age of digital media. There's really no excuse why someone like Marianne Faithfull is unknown to so many. She is a woman who shaped the course of female celebrity, pop stardom, and the British Invasion, and she continues to record and release albums every few years. Her history isn't just for Baby Boomers and perverted old men scrolling YouTube. It is not something to be touted in a *Rolling Stone* "Women of Rock" issue once every decade.

I think about Marianne Faithfull a lot, but she is partially responsible. She is interesting. She is talented, and as a rock music historian, I have a vested interest in women over fifty who are still working and have little time for sentimentality. *Negative Capability* deals almost exclusively with aging, death, love, and loneliness—thoughts that have burdened me since I turned a violent corner into my late thirties and realized that I missed the opportunity to partner up and to tattoo my elbows because the skin has now turned to tissue paper.

I have never met Marianne Faithfull, but I do know that she hates being written about. She reacted negatively to an unauthorized biography, *Marianne Faithfull: As Years Go By*. She called the book "scaly," which I think means snakelike, reptilian, sneaky — something along those lines. I do not want to be scaly. Although part of my job is contingent upon my ability to theorize and postulate about artists, music, and influencers, as a musician myself, a lifelong music fan, an ex-addict, and most likely a bit of a narcissist, I am far more interested in and attuned to how music affects me: personally, physically, emotionally — even psychically. Marianne Faithfull has been one of the great loves of, and great soundtracks to, my life: from a depressed teenager to a homeless addict to a ward of the state (who had a Marianne Faithfull mix cd smuggled into detox) to a functioning, productive, perpetually single, attachment-disordered adult with a sizable Marianne Faithfull record collection.

Faithfull won't talk about her lyrics or discuss her songs in detail. This is a huge pain in the ass for me. But I think being a celebrity, and staying a celebrity, is an extreme way of asking to be understood, whether you enjoy talking to the press and explaining your lyrics or not. Marianne has repeated this desire to be understood in numerous interviews over the years, and I feel guilty as an admirer and fan, afraid that I might not have the right answer, that my theories regarding her lyrics might assume a level of solipsism that isn't really there. I don't think universal understanding exists, but I have an idea about her body of work as it reflects and contributes to my own understanding of my life.

She has told her story, she has been written about, and there was even talk of a Hollywood biopic ten years ago. I am not interested in disputing her truth. I am equally disinterested in presenting myself as an ultimate authority on her or her catalogue or to sling this book as a seminal Marianne Faithfull text. History is subjective, after all. My goal is to present my perspective and to usurp the hierarchical, often carceral gatekeeping inherent in rock writing and scholarship. In doing so, I hope to present a thought-provoking text that encourages curiosity and personal investigation. I am interested in writing about how Faithfull's music makes me feel, about how our lives have intersected, about gender, legacy, and aging. About addiction, survival, relationships, and sleeping with books instead of human beings. About how she's a Capricorn sun and I'm a Capricorn rising, and how I often consider our astrological compatibility. About a widespread cultural amnesia that continues to venerate men as creators of timeless work without considering the intersection of gender in rock 'n' roll culture and history. About how the hell Marianne Faithfull has made it this far.

I

THE "IT GIRL" OF THE
SWINGING SIXTIES

PARENTS

A strange, sometimes fortuitous, sometimes tragic aspect of being a human being is that we are born of parents and exist as a fruit cocktail of their personalities and genes. We are receptacles of inheritance, informed by our environments, experiences, and circumstances. But there's also a mysterious alchemy involved, an alchemy that works to make some people memorable while the rest of us live and die without making much of a splash.

Creativity is genetic. It is also practiced, learned, produced, and cultivated. Marianne's mother, Eva von Sacher-Masoch, was a beautiful Austrian aristocrat with an enviable pedigree. Her great-uncle, Leopold von Sacher-Masoch, authored the novel *Venus in Furs*, which featured a protagonist who yearns to be enslaved and brutalized by the object of his desire. The term "masochism," derived from his name, was coined by Austrian psychiatrist Richard von Krafft-Ebing. Masochism is in Marianne's blood — literally — which might explain the decades-long drug problem.

Eva was a ballerina in Berlin before moving back to her family home in Vienna at the start of World War II. During the war, she edited a popular Austrian magazine called *Wife and Mother* that had been taken over by the Nazis, and she worked to "counter the doctrine it imposed on Austria's women," a feminist act before the concept of feminism existed — and way before it became a bumper sticker.[1] In Marianne's first memoir, she reveals that her mother was raped by a Nazi soldier while hiding in a room at an institute for displaced Hungarians. She murdered the soldier with his own gun before he could do the same to Marianne's grandmother.[2]

Eva met and married Glynn Faithfull in 1945 when they were both thirty-three. A cultured intellectual with a PhD who studied modern languages, Glynn had been a full-time lecturer before joining the intelligence unit of the British army in 1939, where his "main duty was to interrogate prisoners of war."[3] He was enamored of Eva and her family, who were bilingual, cultured, and possessed a kind of "diplomatic privilege" that had protected them throughout the war.[4] It is difficult to piece together what Eva thought of Glynn, but on paper, he was a carbon copy of her father, Artur von Sacher-Masoch, who had been a colonel in World War I and later a writer and philosopher. Eva was warm, emotive, passionate, and volatile while Glynn was detached, dispassionate, and stoic. The relationship disintegrated within a few years, and Eva finally granted Glynn an uncontested divorce in the early 1960s.

He married again in 1963 and had three more children. Eva never remarried.

Trauma is also genetic. A Jewish friend of mine told me that trauma is encoded in the genetic makeup of Holocaust survivors, a phenomenon known as "epigenetics." The horrors of the Holocaust have been passed down from generation to generation, absorbed through the Jewish mother, whose child floats, incubates, in a trauma sac for nine months before being born to repeat the cycle.[5] Marianne Faithfull was born Marian Evelyn Faithfull on December 29, 1946, one year after World War II and one year before the start of the Cold War. Her young life was greatly informed by the effect World War II had on her parents — separation, abandonment, resilience — and her upbringing was very much a result of their experiences during the war. Marianne Faithfull was incubated in a long ancestry of intellectuals, aristocrats, writers, and artists and in the wartime trauma inflicted upon her parents. Subsequently, war, terrorism, relationships, isolation, and love have been lifelong themes in the Marianne Faithfull catalogue, and she has lived her life, in some ways, as a soldier at war with a revolving cast of enemies. At the height of her pop stardom, it was the press and media, the enemy list has always included men and the concept of marriage, then the war was with heroin, and finally, with herself.

Before I agreed to write this book, I mistakenly assumed that she had grown up privileged. As a dumb American, I thought British accents sounded sort of posh. Faithfull, in particular, is known for her distinct elocution. Further investigation into her early life unearthed an interesting bombshell—the pedigree was fact, but the air of aristocracy that her mother continued to cultivate was a myth.

Marianne Faithfull was raised by her mother in a modest home in Reading, England. They were unable to afford extravagances like a telephone, but their home was filled with paintings and mementos representing Eva's familial line. Neighbors recall the family as harmless outcasts who dressed extravagantly and lived a bohemian lifestyle. Her mother threw parties with artists and academics and encouraged Marianne to experience the culture that London had to offer. Loud, opinionated, and creative, Eva was a conspicuous presence in their blue-collar, Catholic neighborhood.

Marianne's father seems to me—and I am as close to a misandrist as a person can get—to have been a self-involved asshole who ditched the family when his daughter was six and contributed very little financially to Marianne's upbringing. She remembers him fondly, probably because he was unavailable and distant and a welcome relief from her mother's volatility and progressive alcoholism. Eva enrolled her in a Roman Catholic primary boarding school as a "subsidized" (charity case) student, against Glynn's wishes. He was a devout atheist and believed that organized religion was a sham. Marianne doesn't seem to have been traumatized by her experience at the convent school, although she does describe it as unpleasant, choosing instead to credit the nuns with instilling a sense of manners and propriety that she has maintained throughout her life. A former professional dancer, Eva overcame the disappointment of not living the life she had imagined for herself by maintaining an air of respectability, living vicariously through her daughter, and later, alcohol and religion.

I'm not sure if it's a character flaw or simply a trait shared by all hardcore music fans and grassroots cultural anthropologists, but when I connect with an artist musically, I search desperately for other commonalities — like growing up poor, being gay, becoming addicted to drugs and alcohol, or being strangely infatuated with whales. Or being the daughter of a single parent. Or being abandoned by fathers and disconnected from volatile mothers.

My biological father is not an intellectual. He never graduated high school and failed both his GED and driver's test multiple times. He was a drug dealer and later a drug addict who impregnated women as a pastime. My mother, in contrast, has always been otherworldly beautiful and very smart. She graduated high school early so she could work and never managed to finish college because she had two kids instead, but everyone assumes she's well educated and I don't correct them. I have no idea what the attraction was between Bio Dad and my mother, but apparently he was into cross dressing, so I guess I know which side the queer gene comes from.

When I was eight, Bio Dad signed some legal documents and rescinded his rights to me and my younger sister, which is sort of fucked up in multiple ways now that I'm an adult. You are born, belonging to people who might not be old enough or mature enough to take care of themselves. You're created, conceived out of a passionate moment, pushed through a wet portal and into the world, branded with a gender, name, family history, and ensuing expectations. My first father couldn't handle the task and forfeited his right to have anything to do with me. My mom met my current dad while she was a waitress at a Chinese restaurant, and after a few months, he decided he wanted the responsibility of a wife and two kids, so we moved to suburban Massachusetts from Poughkeepsie, New York, to start a new life. On moving day, my biological father met us in the parking lot of a convenience store to say goodbye, a moment that is etched in my memory because of its absolute absurdity.

"Ok. See ya," he said as we drove away.

Where Marianne Faithfull and I differ is in our opinions of our fathers and of men in general. I dislike men and their opinions. I dislike how certain men—men like biographers or interviewers—have taken it upon themselves to psychoanalyze women, like Marianne Faithfull, and their relationships with their fathers. I resent how these men are so quick to diagnose "daddy issues" while overlooking women's complicated relationships with all men as a symptom of global patriarchy. In *Marianne Faithfull: As Years Go*

By, biographer Mark Hodkinson concludes that the father-daughter dynamic is the most important one in Marianne Faithfull's life and to understand this is to understand her story.[6] In the introduction of the reissue, he lists the men who "propelled Marianne into such a fantastic life"— literally lists them in the last paragraph and goes on to explain that "most of us consider ourselves lucky to have met one of these influential figures," but how Marianne, you know, paid attention and used these connections to her advantage.[7] It is very hard to take seriously a journalist tasked with researching one of the most important women in rock music history (and it is a very well-researched book), who condenses her legacy down to her ability to work productively with men. This conclusion is outlandishly dismissive. I threw his book across the room—I'm not exaggerating.

If I'm being fair and objective like a good journalist, I would say his perspective is one worth acknowledging and/or investigating, but I also think it is a boring, easy, juvenile perspective. Hodkinson labored over details of her heritage, but his curiosity ends with the facts, lists of intellectuals and aristocrats. He fails to consider how that myth and the pressure to maintain that legacy contributed to Marianne's allure and eventual self-destruction and how her father was the most important relationship in her life because he wasn't there, and it is always easier to fantasize about what's missing than to live with what's in front of you. He also fails to note the implausibility of working in the industry at all in the Swinging Sixties without the help of men. What if we flip the cultural script proposed by Hodkinson and investigate the historical legacy of the muse and why men continue to need her?

I don't know what it's like to be beautiful. I know what it's like to be an acquired taste for some, but largely considered funny, nice, or cute. As I've aged, I've materialized weaponry to deflect male attention and attract the attention of gay women (or straight women interested in expanding their sexual horizons): a monochromatic wardrobe, t-shirts with coded or explicit homosexual/feminist messages, and visible tattoos. I've also just gotten older. Beauty, if you're a woman, is something to overcome, and Marianne Faithfull had to overcome hers like so many other women born into a life of desirability through genetic fluke.

She has always been hot. According to her book of photographs, *Marianne Faithfull: A Life on Record*, she's been beautiful since infancy.[8] At times, she has resented her looks and has even mutilated her face while she was on drugs, but she admits to using it to her advantage throughout her life to gain work, opportunities, and attention. But I think for Marianne Faithfull, being beautiful was more a curse than a blessing because it overshadowed her talent, intelligence, and complexity. Her childhood friend Sally Oldfeld recalled the difficulties Marianne experienced at convent school where she had been marked a scarlet woman by the nuns before entering her teenage years. She was cast into a role and assumed to be "bad" simply because she matured early. Faithfull sought to dispel these projections by being good, to no avail.[9]

Other legendary rocker women — Patti Smith and Joni Mitchell, for instance — are not conventionally attractive and so they have the opportunity to be remembered for their art. Patti Smith wasn't picked out of a crowd at a party and dubbed "an angel with big tits," subsequently having to overcome that title.[10] When Smith married a rock star, the punker Fred Sonic Smith, her entire personal and creative identity did not become subsumed beneath the rubble of their romantic life. Yes, she did disappear from public life for years after her marriage, but her recorded history and current press do not situate her as Fred's widow while Marianne Faithfull continues to be linked, often in headlines, to Mick Jagger and the Stones.

Faithfull's blatant femininity has been a stumbling block on the road to continued historical and cultural relevance. She was too hot to be taken seriously for a long time and has since found the freedom afforded to women who age out of beauty. This is not a negative transition. Becoming invisible to men — or, unfuckable — is a superpower, not a curse. But her beauty, introversion, and perceived superiority were ostracizing traits when she was a child, before her discovery and rise to stardom.

Marianne and her mother stuck out like sore thumbs in their poor Reading neighborhood. Extravagant and outspoken, Eva walked designer dogs in high heels and adopted a local boy, Chris O'Dell, after his parents died.

This was, of course, kind and generous, but it was also scandalous to provincial religious nuts with filthy minds. Chris became the man of the house, but before he came to live with them, Marianne had been an outcast from a single-parent home with "no car, no gramophone, no father."[11] She was described by neighbors as a precocious child—usually code for rude, spoiled, or smart, but mostly a mixture of the three—who wore strange outfits and kept to herself. Marianne was aware of their reputation and spent most of her childhood reading. I don't think being lonely and wanting to fit in are mutually exclusive. She didn't make friends easily because she didn't find her peers interesting, and they found her unapproachable because she was.

Her father remarried when Marianne was a child and had more children, leaving Marianne to feel they had usurped her in her father's affections.[12] Glynn and his family lived at Brazier's Park, a commune of intellectuals and social scientists in Oxfordshire, England. In her first memoir, she describes the commune as a mixture of terrible food, high utopian thoughts, and randy sex.

Like many children of divorce, Marianne was used to act out her parents' resentments. She recalls her mother sending her to Brazier's dressed in extravagant costumes in a ploy to humiliate her modest and frugal ex-husband. Living full-time with Eva, Marianne was accustomed to extravagance, and Glynn constantly complained that she was spoiled. Spoiled with buttered bread, maybe, but certainly not with the affection or the attention of her parents.

She joined a theater company at thirteen, sang folk songs in coffeehouses, and saw plays in London with family friends. An avid reader, she repeated the names Jean-Paul Sartre, Simone de Beauvoir, Louis-Ferdinand Céline, Albert Camus, and Franz Kafka "like catechism" and imitated existentialist icons by imagining herself a misunderstood, tortured genius.[13] She was less precocious, I think, and more curious, a trait that can appear pretentious to people who lack the same intellectual appetite.[14] Marianne and her mother both knew that she would be some kind of artist.

She grew up quickly, as most children of alcoholics do. When she was sixteen, she was invited to a Valentine ball at the University of Cambridge. It was here that she met her future husband and father of her son, John Dunbar. Dunbar was her polar opposite: he smoked pot, hung out with Allen Ginsberg, William S. Burroughs, and Paul McCartney, and knew key players in the 60s music scene. By the time she was seventeen, she was on the road, touring and away from home. She was married with a child by nineteen. At that time, she wanted a conventional life, but instead married a beatnik philosopher and entered the world of pop stardom. This effort to find and maintain balance among her romantic, domestic, and professional lives has remained a continued source of tension. In her autobiography, *Faithfull*, she admits to immediately shooting heroin and having lots of sex the minute she met the Stones and became Mick's girlfriend.[15]

What's interesting about her young life is how she craved the stability of a functioning family structure but also wanted to be respected as an artist and to be able to explore the possibilities of a burgeoning hedonistic decade. She had been left to her own devices as a child—physically left by Glynn and emotionally left by Eva—but had also been kept, like a cat, largely ignored but petted, brushed, encouraged, and touted in public. When she reached pop stardom, the British media treated her the same way; their love was conditional and not to be trusted. She had, however, been instilled with a confidence possessed by only children.[16] I think the most extraordinary gift a parent can give a child is unconditional love, followed by that unwavering belief in self.

THE BRITISH INVASION

The ways that war and popular culture interact are important vehicles for investigating misogyny in the music industry. Marianne Faithfull is the daughter of a mother who had no choice but to resign her creativity and career as a dancer during World War II, and Faithfull came of age in London during the Cold War when gender roles were, once again, being redefined by the state during a long period of postwar recovery. In 1992, comedian George Carlin aptly described war as nothing but "a whole lot of prick waving." The cultural history of the Cold War has been limited to a popular narrative centered on an ideological war between the capitalist United States and the communist Soviet Union. Characterized by fear, paranoia, and jingoism, this war made the working class and innocent civilians collateral damage in a battle of wits between two dick-waving global leviathans.

In America, anti-communist sentiment indoctrinated the public via television, consumer culture, advertising, and the growth of the suburbs. Middle-class, white America was pacified by consumption: suburban houses with white picket fences, household appliances, cars bought on credit and paid for on time, *Leave it to Beaver*, fashion, face creams, and the prospect of achieving the elusive American Dream. Women were coerced and conditioned to stay at home, rein in their sexual urges, raise good citizens, and spend money on items that would make their lives as homemakers easier.

Britain was closer to the lingering devastation of World War II and the implications of the Cold War standoff by virtue of its proximity to European battlefields. To live in Britain in the years following World War II meant living with the physical memory of it in the midst of bombed-out buildings and abandoned military bases. Still, like women in the United States, postwar women in the United Kingdom were not expected to have careers. Those who married and had children or returned to the home after short-term employment benefited from the same modern domestic conveniences as American housewives. Those expectations of contentment with domesticity could explain Marianne Faithfull's ambivalence about marriage and her difficulty sustaining a healthy work/life balance. She internalized her inability to successfully play the part as abject failure, a crime punishable by a decades-long drug addiction.

In both countries, the cultural implications of the Cold War disproportionately affected women, people of color, sexual and gender "deviants" — anyone who strayed from the prototypes of James Bond-esque virile masculinity or

June Cleaver feminine purity, those bodies and characters immune to the communist trap. The nuclear family model not only kept women from working, but also kept them from actively participating in the creative counterculture that blossomed out of Cold War frustrations. The music industry thrived economically in the 1950s and 60s, but it was a direct reflection of the larger misogynistic culture, and it gave female artists like Faithfull little room to grow outside of the pleasant, virginal songstress archetype to which she was initially assigned.

On February 9, 1964, the Beatles, an all-male band from Liverpool, England, performed on *The Ed Sullivan Show* and changed the history of rock music. Their performance brought Beatlemania to North America and marked the first wave of the British Invasion. Following the Beatles' success, English musicians (mostly white, all-male bands) who came to America in the early to mid-1960s found themselves venerated by American kids. Anything English was cool. This applied not only to the bands whose music would stand the test of time, like the Beatles, the Stones, and the Kinks, but also to one-, two-, and three-hit wonders like the Hollies and Herman's Hermits. The Brits' success in America was a beneficial cultural exchange on both sides, putting English music on the map and reinvigorating American music.

The British Invasion was so transformative that it can be seen as the start of the 60s as an era of cultural change.[1] The first musical wave lasted into 1966 and introduced the Beatles, the Rolling Stones, the Animals, the Kinks, the Zombies, the Who, Herman's Hermits, Petula Clark, Lulu, Dusty Springfield, and Marianne Faithfull into the public consciousness. Contrary to popular belief, the Rolling Stones and the Who were failures at first, and it took dozens of attempts for either to chart at all. Both bands, however, were successful members of the second wave, which included Cream, Joe Cocker, Pink Floyd, and the Troggs, all of whom introduced variations of psychedelia and responded to social tensions around the Vietnam War and civil rights. The third, final, and in my opinion, least exciting wave included male-fronted bands Emerson, Lake & Palmer, Thin Lizzy, and Yes. This iteration is partially responsible for the rise of all-male hair metal bands in the 1980s by a generation of listeners who mistook technical competency and boundless soloing as an invitation to just whip their dicks out and objectify women. They really misread the room.

The popular narrative regarding the outcome of the British Invasion leaves little room for criticism. People get attached to their gods and it is almost impossible to separate the underlying context from the well-loved and heavily documented, mostly male, musicians responsible for its continued reverence. The reality, however, is that the British Invasion consisted of white men who were influenced by blues, R&B, and black culture and performed black music for white audiences. Not only that, but the first wave was ushered in on cover songs originally recorded by black artists. For example, the Rolling Stones' self-titled debut album, produced by Andrew Loog Oldham, contained nine cover songs and one original. Eric Burden of the Animals, the Who, and Eric Clapton were all self-professed connoisseurs and interpreters of blues. This commercialized fandom brought public recognition of overlooked black musicians, often at the insistence of their famous white proteges. In 1965, the Rolling Stones agreed to appear on the variety show *Shindig* under the condition that Howlin' Wolf open for the band. This constituted "a life-changing moment, both for the American teenagers clustered round the TV in their living rooms, and for a generation of blues performers who had been stuck in a cultural ghetto."[2]

However, historiography focuses on chart-topping successes. Black musicians never had access to the mainstream while young white men appropriated their music and culture, then commodified and packaged it to appeal to young white audiences who were economically advantaged and able to buy records. Black music remained underground, in black communities, and deeply, yet esoterically, appreciated by record collectors, Anglophiles, and "music nerds." Considering gender, white male musicians were further positioned as experts and sources of coveted musical knowledge while female musicians were written about by white male gatekeepers who prioritized aesthetics.

The economic boom after World War II and technological advancements allowed people to buy things they wanted but didn't need, like records and musical instruments. Boys bought instruments and started bands, but girls were not encouraged to play instruments and were trivialized as screaming admirers or "fangirls." The music industry was similarly aligned with British Cold War respectability and hegemonic femininity. It existed as a microcosm of larger gender inequality while capitalizing on the growing countercultural, anti-establishment ethos of rock music.

All-male bands have been heralded as pioneers of the first wave of the British Invasion with one exception: the Honeycombs, whose claim to fame was their "girl drummer," Honey Lantree. British women were categorized as singer-songwriters like Dusty Springfield, Petula Clark, and Lulu. The American all-girl band, Goldie and the Gingerbreads, had a hit in the United Kingdom in 1965 with "Can't You Hear My Heart Beat." Herman's Hermits had a hit with the same song in the United States, which, according to Gingerbreads lead singer Genya Ravan, would have been preferable as US chart topping was considered the pinnacle of success.[3]

Marianne Faithfull was in the right place, geographically, at the right time, historically speaking, to become the "It Girl" of 1960s Britain. It was a moment of mass consumerism and youth culture and the height of commercial radio. But the industry was an outgrowth of larger Cold War culture and its propagandic sexism. Although her success is regarded differently in America and Europe — she has had more hits in the United Kingdom and in France than in the United States — the prevailing, popular narrative suggests that she is indebted to the Rolling Stones. Of course, her initial break came as a direct result of that relationship, but the opportunities afforded to women were vastly different from those afforded to men, and her collaborations with the Stones were a much-needed stepping-stone into a male-dominated industry.

Having conducted a fair amount of long-form interviews with women-identified musicians, I've become a subscriber to the church of chance. Most of the people I've interviewed didn't have a clear-cut mission or a particular goal. Their paths to success happened organically, without motive, via a willingness to take chances and accept opportunities.

Marianne Faithfull wanted to be a celebrity, but she thought she would be an actress. She was invited to a party when she was seventeen and a naïve convent school student with a boyfriend named John. The Rolling Stones were at this particular party in London, and their manager, Andrew Loog Oldham, targeted her as his next project. Instead of introducing himself to Marianne, he asked her boyfriend if she could sing, and the two men proceeded to have a conversation about her, as if she wasn't there.[4]

Oldham is heralded as a Svengali, a Phil Spector of the British Invasion without the murder conviction. What Oldham and Spector did have in common was the ability to enter into a secret society — rock culture — that catered to men and objectified and commodified women. Oldham succeeded in sculpting a virginal pop icon out of Marianne Faithfull, and when that façade grew tired, he repackaged her as a sex kitten. Faithfull initially found this liberating until she realized the gimmick wasn't intended to free her from the confines of a singular, innocent image. It was intended to sell records. During the British Invasion, she depended on men like Oldham for a career, for money, for navigating the music industry. When she married John Dunbar and had a son, she was no longer of use to Oldham. Even in the Swinging Sixties, being a hot pop star wasn't enough to offset the very unlucrative look of wife and mother. She dated Mick Jagger in the first place — and she has said this on record in the most democratic way possible — out of boredom after being dropped by Andrew the Svengali. Being the girlfriend of a Rolling Stone offered financial security, opportunities to travel the world, and probably served as a passive-aggressive way out of an unsatisfying marriage.

The thing about the popular history of the British Invasion, the Summer of Love, or the 60s in general is that it doesn't account for the bullshit roles women were relegated to within the music scene. I'm not even talking about the business, but about shows, parties, and social gatherings. The history of 60s rock for women certainly includes sex and drugs, and in some cases, fame and fortune, but it excludes the minefield of double standards, sexism, and misogyny that they navigated to achieve even a crumb of success in male-dominated scenes. Faithfull says she was too pretty to be left alone, but she omits the "by men" part. Men like Oldham, no matter how hip, operated in their respective rock 'n' roll settings as reflections of larger sexist, capitalist institutions with all the inequitable trimmings. Marianne Faithfull had to die and come back to life with a different voice in order to achieve a place in rock history.

One of the most poignant passages in Faithfull's 1994 autobiography describes Bob Dylan. I like Bob Dylan. Well, I like his early albums — the ones that he believes, and I'm paraphrasing here, were written by God because the songs are too good for him to have composed on his own. I like *Desire* and the version of "Girl from the North Country" featuring Johnny Cash. I cry my fucking eyes out every time I listen to it. But overall, I think Bob Dylan is overrated, and I think it's ridiculous that he gets standing ovations for despondently grumbling into a microphone and berating his audience. I do believe, however, that he was a conduit for some higher power at a particular moment in history and that he wrote highly regarded, important albums during that time that spawned a lot of cheap imitations in their aftermath.

Marianne described Bob in a way I would have assumed: stoned, egotistical boy genius composing poems on a typewriter in the middle of parties. I also wasn't surprised to learn that he had a crush on Faithfull and employed all of the corny band-guy tactics to get her to bed, like acting mysterious, writing her a song, insulting her—you know, the usual. What I found unbearably depressing was his treatment of Joan Baez. There's this part where she shows up at one of these parties in London and starts playing a song. Faithfull recalls Bob insulting her, imitating her, glaring at her, and embarrassing her in front of an adoring audience. And Baez never said anything.[5] She ignored him, maybe left the room. It must have hurt. But this is the point: There wasn't some set-in-stone rule that you couldn't tell Bob Dylan to shut the fuck up, but nobody told him to do anything. Women tolerated his attitude or his flirtations because it was important to be in that room with those people.

At the risk of making broad sweeping generalizations, I will say that being a woman in music means navigating various iterations, expressions, and levels of how Marianne Faithfull and Joan Baez were treated by Bob Dylan. This navigation occurs across genres, over time, and throughout history. Gender remains a useful category of analysis thirty-plus years after Joan Scott proclaimed it so in 1986.[6] Theoretical approaches aside, it is also a personal category of analysis that directly affects women, transgender, and gender-nonconforming individuals in day-to-day life. This is the reason I am highly attuned to women in music; we have all experienced misogyny—some of us in the music industry, some of us in our local music scenes. Although the definition of gender has evolved, it is a salient component to personal, lived experience and identity formation. A generation after Marianne Faithfull's experience with sexism in the music industry, it remained alive and well in the suburbs of the northeastern United States and predicated my eventual career as a protector of women's histories.

I joined my first band, Thriftshop Apocalypse, in high school. The 1990s were great for mainstream women in rock, but that gender inclusivity did not translate to our small suburban town. We were the only girls in a band in my high school, and we played rock music taken straight from a 90s alternative blueprint. I think that is what musical exploration is: stealing bits and pieces of people's stuff and making it your own, discovering who you really are in the process. Boys, for the most part, have a head start by being introduced to rock culture early on. All of the boys in bands in my high school had been playing instruments far longer than we had, and they possessed what seemed to me at the time to be a genius level of musical knowledge. They were nice to our faces because our lead singer was popular and hot and our drummer was seriously good, but I was ridiculed daily in Latin class for my taste and t-shirts and asked what it was like to be in a band with the hottest girl in school as I picked lunch remnants out of my braces.

I discovered punk after graduation and started a band with a group of male friends. Because I was still a closeted virgin at nineteen with no viable romantic options, I thought it was reasonable to date my best friend and bandmate. (Side note: being a girl in an all-male band means that a few of them will drunkenly profess their love to you at some point. This is awkward and unprofessional but usually pretty easy to diffuse or ignore.) I lost my virginity to my best friend and bandmate in the back of his car. My only memory of the experience is that it was painful and hot. This was followed by a crushing sense of dread upon realizing the significance that a penis inserted into a vagina holds for young men. He was instantaneously in love with me and I was disgusted. The thing about being gay is that you can't become un-gay. And the thing about being the only girl in an all-male band who breaks up with her boyfriend/bandmate is that the girl is labeled a tease, or a whore and a bitch, and is exiled from the group. This was my introduction to the weaponization of women's sexual autonomy.

When I was twenty, I went to a guitar store to purchase my first real Fender—an embarrassingly extravagant purchase so close to Christmas, but I really wanted it. I walked inside and was welcomed by a young male employee with a ponytail who obviously knew his way around "Stairway to Heaven" and promptly asked if I was shopping for my boyfriend.

In my early thirties, I decided to pursue a graduate degree in history, which is quite a male-dominated field, but I decided to document rock music, which is also a male-dominated field. In 2015, I participated in a panel at a punk conference on the East Coast. I explained that I avoided white male historians in an attempt to create a more diverse knowledge base in my own studies and to be able to situate my work within a context more relatable to me and to the people whose histories I document. At the end of the day, the keynote speaker, a grown man and respected scholar, thanked me from the podium for staying around and listening to "all of the boring white men," like a toddler tattling on me in front of his friends. You don't have to be famous to deal with these kinds of men. They transcend time and space and leave waves of eager and tenacious women in their wake, generation after generation.

My relationship to music, and to Marianne Faithfull in particular, exists at a crossroads — an intersection of multiple identities as an ever-aging, white, cis-gendered woman, a lesbian, and a recovered alcoholic. It's no secret that we, marginalized music listeners and fans, search for representations of ourselves in popular culture. The elusiveness of these outsider identities birthed scholarship, books, and studies dealing with what are still largely considered niche categories and even brand-new subfields within the larger fields of history, gender, and cultural studies. As Jodie Taylor points out: "[P]opular music has figured centrally in the fashioning of queer identities and self-consciousness, 'merg[ing] queer social relations with queer musical ones, thus demonstrating the transforming significance of musical discourses.'"[7] But before I knew all this information, which unfortunately remains inaccessible to those without access to higher education, I felt acutely, devastatingly alone. I felt alone as a gay person, as an addict, and as a girl in a band.

Popular music has figured centrally in fashioning identities, and this was true for me, a daydreaming kid in the suburbs, mainlining all the information I could get about women rock musicians—the more abrasive, the better. I felt that my "queerness"—my sexuality; my disinterest in relationships, marriage, and children; and my general discontent with my allocated position at the bottom of the musical hierarchy—was best represented in the form of alcoholic torch singers and John Waters-esque, shit-eating irreverence. Marianne Faithfull dressed in a nun's habit, singing "I Got You Babe" with David Bowie; Judy Garland's emotive delivery of traditional standards to hordes of fawning gay men; L7's cheeky political feminism; Marianne in a black suit on *Saturday Night Live*, singing backup vocals for a metal band—these visuals brought me relief.

This need to see ourselves in larger culture doesn't only apply to us normal, average people. Connection is a necessary condition of human nature. Faithfull rose to fame at a time when famous women were anomalies whose success was contrived and built on specific, male-curated attributes. In Marianne's case, these were her looks, her virginity, and her voice. She existed very much on her own, with few female peers, and no one she could relate to on a personal or professional level.

In 2002, she wrote "Song for Nico," which appears on the album *Kissin' Time*. The lyrics illustrate how the need for representation and kindred spirits extends beyond fandom and into the realm of legends who made their way alone in predominantly male fields:

> And now she doesn't know what it is she wants
> And where she wants to go
> And will Delon be still a cunt
> Yes, she's in the shit, though she is innocent

Faithfull never met Christa Paffgen, better known as Nico, but they lived parallel lives. Both were discovered by men and both reached a level of celebrity because they were beautiful but also possessed a morbid intensity and artistry that displaced them from the burden of expectations and commodification. In 1962, Nico gave birth to her son, Ari, a product of her affair with the actor Alain Delon. Delon denied paternity — although the resemblance is uncanny — and when Nico plunged into heroin addiction, Ari was raised by his paternal grandmother who maintained a close relationship with Nico. In 1968, Marianne co-starred with Delon in *The Girl on a Motorcycle*. He played the object of her desire and the subject of her psychedelic, sexual fantasies. Marianne Faithfull has called Nico an underestimated and misunderstood artist whose life has been reduced to the "troubled life bit," an assessment that Marianne could easily attribute to her own life and musical legacy. She identified with Nico's frustration at not being given the opportunity to fully express herself—especially in her work with the Velvet Underground. "She was underestimated, and now she's dead. Who's going to stand up for her? Me!"[8]

POP STARDOM

Marianne Faithfull's childhood didn't last very long. She met the Rolling Stones' manager, Andrew Loog Oldham, in 1964 when she was seventeen and he was twenty. When I think about rock history or the people who have contributed to it, I think of them as adults. In reality, at the start of their careers, many were barely old enough to drink, and in many cases, their careers were over, or they were dead, before thirty.[1] Two days after she met him at a party, Marianne brought her acoustic guitar to Andrew's office and sang folk songs for him—a kind of makeshift audition—although he had already determined her future for her.

> The minute I saw Marianne I knew she was something special . . . she had this fantastic virginal look. I mean, at the time when most chicks were shaking ass and coming on strong, here was this pale, blonde, retiring, chaste teenager looking like the Mona Lisa, except with a great body. I didn't care whether she could sing or not, I could sell that look, and I'd learned what miracles could be achieved by clever engineers in a recording studio.[2]

Oldham had presented the Rolling Stones as the bad boy antithesis of the Beatles, and he needed an act that would balance out his growing roster. A cunning businessman, he hoped to create a combination that would provide "an effective insurance policy against fluctuating trends."[3] He was also determined to make Mick Jagger and Keith Richards a songwriting team to rival Paul McCartney and John Lennon. Singers like Dionne Warwick and Dusty Springfield had chart success, and Oldham imagined Marianne Faithfull as a useful tool: In becoming part of this growing trend of successful female singers, she could help him make a name for himself as the next Phil Spector. In 1964, Oldham recruited Mick and Keith to write a song for Marianne, and the result was the sad, introspective ballad, "As Tears Go By." The song's sentiment complemented her young, virginal image and created a unique juxtaposition to the upbeat pop songs heralded by emerging girl singers of the British Invasion.[4]

It is the evening of the day
I sit and watch the children play
Smiling faces I can see
But not for me

Oldham's theory of pop was rooted in image. He knew the kind of character he wanted Marianne to play—a continuation of the naïve, ex-convent schoolgirl—and he tasked Mick and Keith with writing a song specifically for her that would conjure the image of a young beautiful girl trapped behind high convent walls. Legend has it that Oldham locked Richards and Jagger in a kitchen and when they emerged, "As Tears Go By" was finished. Within weeks, it became Marianne's first number one hit and propelled her into celebrity life.[5]

Faithfull attributes the trajectory of her career, and her longevity, to her willingness to take opportunities. She joined the British major label, Decca Records, during one of its most successful and prolific decades. "As Tears Go By" first appeared on the charts in summer 1964. It debuted at number twenty-seven after weeks of press and marketing negotiated by Oldham with the intention of inundating the public with its new pop princess. Peter Jones, the first journalist to interview the Beatles, was also the first to interview Marianne for his weekly column in *Record Mirror*, under the headline "Marianne Is a 'Real' Nice Person."[6] Before the interview, Oldham insisted that Jones play up the innocent, convent girl stereotype. In an early television performance for *Hullabaloo*, a short-lived series showcasing British and American folk and R&B performers, Marianne lip-synched "As Tears Go By." Perched demurely yet seductively on a pedestal, she wore a white dress, personifying the virginal image and embodying both Oldham's vision for her and the sentiment of the song.

While the image of a naïve, nubile young goddess was being formed in the media, Marianne began traveling for promotional trips, experimenting with drugs, and enjoying sex with a variety of partners. She had her first lesbian relationship with a sixteen-year-old girl named Saida after taking a sedative. "You see, I've lived a sheltered life with the convent schooling and so on. Now I'm getting a chance to meet 'real' people, outside, if you see what I mean."[7]

Because Marianne was underage, Eva Faithfull had to sign the contract Oldham had drawn up for her. Marianne and her mother viewed pop stardom as a means to an end, a way to make money, and a brief diversion from her destiny as a serious actress or artist. But Marianne also felt abandoned by her mother, sold to the highest bidder, and left to navigate a strange new world on her own. After the success of "As Tears Go By," Oldham put Marianne on a weekly wage of eighty pounds, three times more than men working white-collar jobs at the time.[8] She was a "Dedicated Follower of Fashion"[9] long before her friendship with supermodel Kate Moss and trips to Paris Fashion Week. She spent money frivolously, commissioned clothing from designers, bought cars, and moved out of her mother's house and into a London flat. She spent 1964 recording and traveling on popular package tours made up of dozens of acts that traveled by bus to various destinations throughout Britain. These tours were brutal, poorly organized money-making ventures and physical manifestations of the greed that grew out of the pop business in the 1960s. Marianne survived a grueling schedule and squalid accommodations by fucking on the road, drinking, and taking drugs. She had an abortion in fall 1964, a result of one of these "tour affairs," and her boyfriend John Dunbar, in a state of panic, proposed marriage in December, shortly before her eighteenth birthday.

Catholic guilt is a helluva drug. In Mark Hodkinson's biography, *Marianne Faithfull: As Years Go By*, she discusses the dilemma of coming of age on a tour bus: "I saw myself as a good girl and suddenly I was being very promiscuous. . . . I started to think I was a bad woman, a whore and a slut. I'd better get married and then I'd be good again."[10] She was already pregnant when she married John Dunbar in spring 1965, and they honeymooned in Paris with Allen Ginsberg and a group of Beat poets. She maintained her rigorous schedule and recorded and released her highest-charting hit, "Come and Stay With Me," in February 1965. The song was written for Marianne by singer-songwriter Jackie DeShannon, whose track record includes hits like "What the World Needs Now Is Love" and "Put a Little Love in Your Heart."

> Lovers of the past I'll leave behind
> There'll never be another on my mind
> I'll do all I can so you'll feel free
> If you come and stay with me

During that same *Hullabaloo* appearance in 1965, she performed "Come and Stay With Me." Only this time, she stood up, perfectly still, legs crossed at the ankles and her arms motionless at her sides. Faithfull's voice, at this stage in her career, was pretty but otherwise unremarkable. It was breathy and feminine with a delicate natural vibrato perfectly suited for the formulaic blend of folk and pop that Oldham believed would make her a star. Lyrically, "Come and Stay With Me" predetermined her relationship with Mick Jagger and what she would give up for him in the name of love. In 1965, she was singularly a pop singer and a style icon. She sang songs that were written for her and enjoyed being young and rich, although motherhood and marriage hadn't lived up to her expectations.

Marianne wanted to record a folk album, but Decca wanted a pop album. They reached a compromise, and in April 1965, Faithfull released two debut albums: *Come My Way*, a folk album, and *Marianne Faithfull*, a pop album. It was a genius marketing strategy that offered something for everyone. It is important to note that early in her career, music was a means to an end, a way to support herself and her family. She was a singer who did not invest herself in songwriting or consider herself a musician or an artist in her own right. In October that same year, she released an orchestral version of Paul McCartney's song, "Yesterday." She performed it with Paul during a televised special while she was eight months pregnant, a brazen move at a time when pregnant women were rarely seen on television lest viewers consider women human beings with sexual impulses. Shortly after giving birth prematurely to her son, Nicholas, on November 10, 1965, she announced a six-month break from the pop business. She was nineteen years old, a celebrity, one of the most successful female musicians in Britain, and a wife and mother. Faithfull released three more albums for Decca between 1965 and 1967 — *Go Away from My World*, *North Country Maid*, and *Love in a Mist* — but she would not record another studio album until 1976.

Faithfull was not destined to become a stage actress. Her name is proof enough that she was meant for rock stardom. With a name like Marianne Faithfull, she could only be a musician or a porn star. She started her acting career in Reading as a member of the Progress Theatre's Student Group in the early 1960s as a way to practice her craft and meet boys. Her mother assumed Marianne would be an artist and encouraged her daughter's creative pursuits.[11] She was so encouraging, in fact, that Marianne believed that Eva had in effect sold her to Andrew Loog Oldham, although she has since come to terms with her resentment.[12] Mothers do have a tendency to live through their children. Especially if they feel, as Eva did, shortchanged or cheated in their own lives. Marianne took acting seriously while other kids treated it like a hobby. It gave her a vague inkling about her place in the world as an interpreter of words and a purveyor of feelings.

I have a thing for the French director, Jean-Luc Godard. Almost all his films make me want to fall miserably in love or die — except for his 1966 film *Made in the U.S.A.*, which is too boring to elicit a response. Its only redeeming quality is a diner scene in which Marianne sings "As Tears Go By" in a booth. She made a more memorable film appearance in the 1967 *I'll Never Forget What's'isname*, playing the often-nude, foul-mouthed friend of the protagonist. In 1968, Faithfull became a cult hero as the sexy, leather-clad biker in *The Girl on a Motorcycle*. She plays a bored suburban housewife who embarks on a quest to find a former lover, recalling the events leading up to her escape in a series of psychedelic flashbacks. Along the way, she is touched inappropriately by strange men and sexually harassed periodically.

In April 1967, Marianne returned to the theater, playing Irina in Anton Chekhov's *Three Sisters* at the Royal Court. In an interview with the *Guardian*, she blames her extended absence on the demands of her "pop manager," who wouldn't allow it. The character Irina is the youngest of the three Prosozov sisters, a kind and benevolent person who believes that a good life is the reward of hard work. This role was not unlike Marianne's critically acclaimed performance in the 2007 film, *Irina Palm*, about a grandmother who resorts to sex work to save her grandson's life.

In 1969, Marianne was cast as Ophelia in Tony Richardson's production of *Hamlet* at the Roundhouse in London. Shakespeare's Ophelia is a beautiful young woman, the daughter of Polonius, and the love interest of Hamlet. Hamlet's distrust, manipulation, and perverting of Ophelia's innocence ultimately drives her to suicide. At the time of the filming, Marianne was a heroin addict having an affair of convenience with the Rolling Stones' drug dealer, Tony Sanchez. She would shoot up during intermission, then reappear on stage, a viscerally defeated, raving mad flower child. In her 1994 autobiography, she explains her reasons for accepting the role and the implications it had on her life:

> For years I had been babbling about death in interviews. That was playacting. There came a time, however, that it stopped being a performance. The combined effect of playing Ophelia and doing heroin induced a morbid frame of mind—to say the least—and I began contemplating drowning myself in the Thames. I was acting as a child does. I had fused with my part. . . . I would indulge myself in lurid pre-Raphaelite fantasies of floating down the Thames with a garland of flowers around my head.[13]

Her acting roles in the 1960s, particularly *The Girl on a Motorcycle* and Ophelia, were polarizing, and she received mixed reviews. By that point, her image solidified around the scarlet letter she had been anointed with at convent school and carried into pop stardom, and there was little chance that she could play any role outside of it. As her drug use progressed, her acting career went downhill, and she was offered fewer and fewer parts until the offers stopped altogether.

Much like the sexy stifled housewife in *The Girl on a*

Motorcycle, Marianne was bored, trapped, and exhausted by 1966. Her London home had become a sort of den of iniquity and shooting gallery for her husband and his intellectual junkie friends. She was disappointed with the reality of her marriage, motherhood, and the fallacious promises of the 60s, as these seemed to cater exclusively to men like her husband. She romanticized the world of drugs in an attempt to escape her situation and sought to imitate personal icons, Aldous Huxley, William Blake, Lewis Carroll, and later the Beats, particularly William S. Burroughs. She partied and wandered around London, returning to the apartment every four hours to breast-feed, a physical manifestation of her internal conflict, one experienced by many women who felt shortchanged by the promises of marriage and motherhood at a time when it seemed like the world was opening up. But she was also nineteen years old. I couldn't properly take care of my cat when I was nineteen, let alone sustain a career and raise a family.

BREASTS

I watched *The Girl on a Motorcycle* recently to contemplate her boobs under that iconic tight leather jumpsuit. I consider Marianne Faithfull's breasts to be important vehicles in her overall legacy. They played a part in her discovery, boosted her pop career, and made a space for her in a male-dominated scene. Her breasts created the exposure for her talent and brought her due respect in the industry.

This is, no doubt, a gendered interpretation, but an interpretation worth considering. There is a fear that women resign their seriousness if they acknowledge their femininity or explicit experiences outside the realm of hypermasculine rock 'n' roll culture. Many women in rock are mothers, for instance. Many have great tits that afforded them certain opportunities and certainly created a route to success that would be vastly different from, say, a flatchested butch lesbian singer or a cis man. The current gender revolution complicates this idea, but it doesn't negate the fact that women have experiences that diverge from the traditional rock narrative. Maybe looking at Marianne Faithfull's history through the lens of her breasts would add more insight into her personal history as an artist and performer, her "inconsistent" catalogue, and her Rock & Roll Hall of Fame absence.

A titty-centered analysis of her career begs acknowledging a gender binary, which I will use because her career began at a time of strict binaries and clearly defined gender relations in the 1960s. Marianne's boobs have affected the development of her career for more than fifty years and continue to affect her ability to achieve the level of cultural and social relevance and economic security afforded her peers — specifically, men. Unfortunately for Marianne, it's less about the tits and more about her brand of femininity. She was discovered because of her boobs (and the rest of her body), her beauty, her seeming agreeable nature, and naivete. Subsequent opportunities were made available to her because of her marketability, i.e., her looks, her boobs, and her willingness to comply. She toured extensively, until she exhausted herself, and wasn't particularly demanding of her managers or handlers. She gradually became a style icon and public figure during the Swinging Sixties, roles inextricably linked to her body, youth, and femininity. But Mick Jagger didn't want her once she had gained fifty pounds and the *Daily Mail* infamously fat shamed her in 2012 when she was sixty-five years old.[1] Faithfull was given the space and opportunity to perform her femininity and to expose her breasts (to zip and unzip that black leather jumpsuit)[2] until the Redlands drug bust in 1967. Her perceived sexual autonomy became entangled with the growth of a perceptibly dangerous, drug-taking hippie culture that the Establishment sought to suppress. One of the most repeated myths about that police raid at Keith Richards's home is that she deliberately exposed herself to detectives, a story she emphatically denies.

Her development as an artist, since the comeback period, has been rooted in an image and in historical memory, informed by her tits and what they meant and stood for during an important cultural and musical moment. Her boobs are harbingers of nostalgia, but most importantly, they are instruments of a kind of abject femininity unrewarded by rock culture or its institutions. A gender- or tits-centered analysis fails to implicate tastemakers who disregard varying expressions of femininity—women's bodies, blonde hair, big boobs—as vehicles of valid, authentic art. And while hegemonic expressions of femininity are marketable, as evidenced in Marianne's early career, she perverted that archetype by behaving like her hard-partying male colleagues. And although rock music and culture are grounded in disrupting convention, Marianne Faithfull and her blonde hair and great tits have had to navigate a lifetime of double standards. She has had to work twice as hard achieve a portion of the economic gains, social, cultural, and historical relevance that men in rock are so generously afforded.

Much has been written about the technophallus, or guitars as phallic extensions of the male rock body, and how this Big Dick Energy is integral to the nature of rock 'n' roll.[3] This kind of ahistoricism serves to diminish the authenticity of women's rock performance and works to further invalidate expressions of femininity within rock culture. But it also radicalizes the prospect of seriously analyzing breasts, and rock history is full of them.

I love boobs. My end-of-life care plan includes death by cleavage, via heavenly suffocation, so I have considered their purpose beyond feeding children and personal enjoyment. It is interesting to consider how these appendages have been used as instruments of patriarchal control even within countercultural scenes or during supposed progressive historical moments, like the free-loving Swinging Sixties, and how gender analyses are complicated and nuanced—and maybe a bit arbitrary. But it's also interesting to consider how using Marianne Faithfull's tits as a legitimate method of analysis to investigate her career, her legacy, and gender relations in the music industry in the 1960s can work to expand upon an androcentric historical rock context. Breasts have the power to suffocate the technophallus.

"WILD HORSES COULDN'T DRAG ME AWAY"

Marianne Faithfull and Mick Jagger didn't start their iconic relationship immediately after they crossed paths at that party in 1964. They were each engaged to others, and the Rolling Stones hadn't reached their peak yet — they were unhip and maybe even a little embarrassing. Once she began her career and started frequenting their orbit, Marianne preferred Keith, whom she found effortlessly cool and a gentleman, while Mick was lewd, a bit of a poseur, and a showman. She slept with Keith and spent a lot of time doing drugs with Brian Jones and Anita Pallenberg. When she finally responded to Mick's advances, the relationship happened organically. He accompanied her to Italy where she was scheduled to appear at the San Remo Music Festival in 1967. She fell in love with Mick during a storm:

[T]hey hired a boat to sail on the Mediterranean, docking overnight in Nice and Villefranche-sur-Mer. The boat was shared with a crew of two and a nanny to take care of Nicholas. During a storm, Marianne, Jagger and Nicholas climbed into a bunk and held one another, waiting for the storm to pass.[1]

There's a joke about lesbians renting U-Hauls on their second date, and we do have a tendency to race toward some invisible finish line, but rock stars might be worse. Marianne moved into Mick's place in 1967 when they returned from Italy, leaving Nicholas with a nanny. Once the two had merged their lives, Marianne started to disappear as an individual and as a performer. Her last album with Decca, the 1966 *North Country Maid*, failed to chart while the Rolling Stones reached global super stardom with the release that same year of *Aftermath*. It's not that Mick Jagger asked her to stop working, insisting that she follow his band around instead, but that Marianne had been under the assumption that her career was trivial from the beginning. She was twenty-one years old in 1967, and the mother of a two-year-old son. Although caustic about her reasons for entering into a relationship with Mick Jagger and about the depth of their intensity and devotion, she did love him. But her decision was also financial. Being Mick Jagger's girlfriend was a more guaranteed investment than continuing to pursue her career as an independent musician. And then the Redlands drug bust happened, which pretty much sealed her fate.

Redlands was Keith Richards's home in West Wittering, Sussex, and the drug bust was a setup in which Marianne was collateral damage yet suffered the greatest fallout.

Mick had brought a libel suit against a newspaper, *News of the World*, that wrongly labeled him a user of LSD. Marianne has described Mick as a narc on more than one occasion and someone who hung around drug users to maintain his bad boy image but rarely used drugs himself. Instead of apologizing or retracting their statements, the newspaper decided to substantiate the rumor, setting up a drug bust with the help of Keith's driver. There were drugs in the house, in people's systems, in briefcases and bags, but the party was, by all accounts, tame when the police arrived. Unfortunately for Marianne, she had taken her clothes off and bathed after a walk in the woods and was wrapped in a large rug when the police entered.

Celebrity culture was one unfortunate result of the Swinging Sixties/British Invasion. The media frenzy that followed the Redlands bust is similar to the paparazzi/ TMZ celebrity takedowns of today. Marianne was a pop star whose image had been teetering on a precipice — having left her husband for Mick Jagger and become a rather unfit mother — and being the lone, nude woman at a Rolling Stones drug party was all the media needed to destroy her. Once news of the rug reached the public, another ridiculous story materialized: Mick had been eating a Mars bar out of her vagina at the time of the bust. (Anyone who has ever performed cunnilingus knows that a candy bar in a vagina is ridiculous and unnecessary. A vagina is nature's candy bar.) Although Marianne was not convicted of a crime, her morality was most certainly on trial. And while the Rolling Stones became freedom fighters in the wake of this well-orchestrated attack at the hands of the Establishment, she was unable to shed the stain of immorality that clung to her like a scarlet letter.[2]

> The Mars Bar was a very effective piece of demonizing. Way out there. It was so overdone, with such malicious twisting of the facts. Mick retrieving a Mars Bar from my vagina, indeed! It was far too jaded for any of us even to have conceived of. It's a dirty old man's fantasy — some old fart who goes to a dominatrix every Thursday afternoon to get spanked. A cop's idea of what people do on acid![3]

In a matter of four years, Marianne was transformed from virginal pop princess to defamed junkie whore. After Redlands, her relationship with Mick deteriorated while her drug addiction accelerated in response to a series of personal tragedies and professional disappointments. In 1968, she and Mick announced they were expecting their first child together, but Marianne miscarried a daughter, Corrina, two months before she was scheduled to give birth. Her last attempt at recording until 1976 happened in 1969 when Decca, desperate for new material, released *The World of Marianne Faithfull*, a compilation album. They pushed the single "Something Better," and Marianne recorded a B-Side, "Sister Morphine," a song she co-wrote with Mick.

I think musicians, famous or not, have a tendency to

determine their futures or their fates with their music, whether they like it or not. If the law of attraction exists, it would make sense. You're repeating your intentions in the recording studio, on stage, in your bedroom — wherever — until eventually you start to live the overall sentiment. I remember when Hole's *Live Through This* came out in 1994 after Kurt Cobain's suicide, and Courtney Love commented on what an odd and unfortunate premonition the whole thing was. Likewise, "Sister Morphine" was a portent of the overdose that would put Marianne in a coma in 1969.

> Here I lie in my hospital bed
> Tell me, sister morphine, when are you coming 'round
>   again?
> Oh, I don't think I can wait that long
> Oh, you see that my pain is so strong

Once the label actually listened to the lyrics, which reference drug taking, they withdrew the record and ceased production. She parted ways with the label shortly after. The censorship fight with Decca preceded a full career halt. Meanwhile, the Rolling Stones included "Sister Morphine" on their album *Sticky Fingers* in 1971, without a problem, proving the different rules in place for men and women in the industry at the time. The Stones did not give her songwriting credit until the album was re-released in 1994.[4] In *Marianne Faithfull: As Years Go By*, she describes the effect the "Sister Morphine" double standard had on her career, her self-worth, and her relationship with Jagger:

> I could see that the champion and the winner of the rock 'n' roll stakes was going to be Mick. I could never compete. I would just have to accept my fate and be Mick's muse. The role of a muse is one of the acceptable ones for women, but it's terrible.[5]

The dictionary defines the word "muse" as "a person — especially a woman — who is a source of artistic inspiration. In mythology, the Muses were nine goddesses who symbolized the arts and sciences. Today, a muse is a person who serves as an artist's inspiration." Although the muse has been redefined as a genderless source of artistic inspiration, it's hard to separate the word from its gendered history. Remnants of its feminine origins can still be found in popular culture today, from *Annie Hall* to the tired Manic Pixie Dream Girl trope. Male muses are few and far between. To delegate the man to the role of muse is a form of castration — a crime against nature really — that would defy social order.

The problem, though, is not the muse. It is the gendered restrictions placed on them. When Faithfull abnegated her own needs to be in a relationship with Mick Jagger, it was a reasonable choice to make because it aligned with their predetermined roles. Had Mick retired to support Marianne's career, this would be a very different book. The image of the gendered muse is dangerous because it denies women their humanity and agency in the artistic process. The muse becomes a passive receptacle for male genius, defined by him rather than by her own creative expression. Faithfull was a victim of the bifurcation of genius into the gendered master/muse binary, which has thrived because we are socially conditioned to accept genius men and question genius women. We would have fewer genius men without the gendered muse, though. Men need muses in order to create. They are not encouraged or socially conditioned toward self-reflection, emotionality, and deep insight. If they are white, they are also born into positions of social, cultural, and political power and are by nature less inclined to express frustration or discontent through artistic processes. In short, men need muses because men are boring.

Another repercussion of the double standard revealed with the release of "Sister Morphine" is Faithfull's hesitancy to embrace personal or confessional lyrics. Memoir and personal experience are attributed to sentimentality, frivolity — that is, femininity. This feminization of memory and memoir and the masculinization of fact, storytelling, and true "art" mirrors larger structural inequalities that continue to contribute to a lasting gender discrepancy in music history. There's a dismissive tone that people often take when they're talking about memoirs by women that serves to diminish them. But when men tell a personal story, it is seen as an act of bravery.

Faithfull released another version of "Sister Morphine" on *Broken English* and has since recorded and performed the song, giving different backstories as to its origin: It's about a man in a hospital after a car accident or a drug dealer she discovered dead in his apartment after an overdose. Or, she says, it's a simple story—women can tell stories, too. But, most poignantly, she has admitted, "All of my songs are about me."[6] During a recorded performance in Los Angeles in 2005, before launching into "Sister Morphine," Faithfull explained to a rapt audience, "I don't write messages; I write stories."[7] She hadn't performed the song live in years, and it was the second time she mentioned Jagger—he wrote the music and she wrote the lyrics.

It's pretty obvious, given Marianne Faithfull's history with drug addiction and near-death experiences that "Sister Morphine" reflects some amount of her lived experience. And why shouldn't it? Would "Sister Morphine" be less valuable if it was a first-person account? If the answer is yes, it's important to ask why, and the answer to that question is rooted in decades of criticisms directed at women's experience, criticisms that have created erroneous assumptions about gender and have defined memory and experience as inconsequential, lesser forms of artistic expression. The feminization of genres, styles, and methods are cultural constructions proliferated by media. Men tell personal stories and they're heroic. Women tell personal stories and they're overindulgent. But, no, personal stories and memoiric lyrics are not inherently feminine, and femininity is not inherently inauthentic, and "Sister Morphine" might just be a little bit about Marianne Faithfull, and that is just fine.

In 1969, Marianne began injecting heroin instead of smoking it, an economical, less wasteful way to use. She also began sleeping with her drug dealer, another cost-cutting measure. She was cast alongside Mick in the film *Ned Kelly*, as his on-screen sister, Maggie Kelly, playing a subordinate role although she was a more experienced actor. And in a crushing personal blow, her friend and Rolling Stone Brian Jones died of a drug-related drowning in summer 1969. Marianne saw herself in Brian — they were both exceptionally smart, curious, and both lacked the physical and mental constitution to work in the music business and control their drug consumption. She watched Brian disintegrate, and anorexic, depressed, and addicted to heroin, she followed suit.

During the filming of *Ned Kelly*, shortly after Brian's death and memorial concert, Marianne overdosed on one hundred and fifty sleeping tablets prescribed by her doctor. She fell into a coma, unable to leave the hospital for nearly a month, under the care of her mother. She awoke to Mick at her side. He told her she almost died, and legend has it that she responded with "wild horses couldn't drag me away," which later became the title of a Rolling Stones hit.

Childhood living is easy to do
The things you wanted I bought them for you
Graceless lady you know who I am
You know I can't let you slide through my hands

In 1970, Marianne ended her relationship with Mick, not, contrary to popular belief, the other way around. Because she was an addict, she attempted to quit heroin with barbiturates and alcohol. That same year, her divorce from John Dunbar was finalized, and shortly after, the twenty-three-year-old Marianne was engaged to Lord Patrick "Paddy" Rossmore, a forty-three-year-old architectural photographer who lived with his mother. He gifted her a copy of William Blake's *Songs of Innocence and of Experience* (like her father had) and paid for her to be injected with valium twice a week.

Marianne has commented on Mick's narcissism—how she felt that he loved her, but that his love was conditioned on her remaining beautiful, pliable, and subordinate. She has made broader statements about men in rock, noting that women are welcomed as muses, mothers, sexual objects, and drug buddies and are no longer of use once they acquire some independence, a drug habit, or sobriety. Marianne, in the middle of her addiction, having separated herself from Mick Jagger, entered a relationship with a seemingly well-intentioned man who paid for her to be medically subdued on a weekly basis. Albert Einstein once defined insanity as doing the same thing over and over and expecting different results. Marianne's determination to be partnered, to play house, to find a man who would take care of her always ended in disappointment or chaos. The storybook romances were secondary to her drug use and her career aspirations and more of a projection of her tenuous relationship with her father than a well-articulated, heartfelt goal.

In her first autobiography, *Faithfull*, Marianne describes the last experience she had with Mick before he gave up on her. He had continued to call, write, and keep in touch long after they had broken up, pleading to see her in person. She had gained fifty pounds from a diet of alcohol during the Paddy recovery period. She continued to gain weight, intentionally, and cut her hair before agreeing to meet with Mick in London in 1972. Her recollection is that he took one look at her, "a look of utter horror," and the phone calls and letters stopped immediately.[8] After ending her engagement to Paddy and the ill-fated meeting with Mick, she lived with a Parisian drug dealer to the stars, who beat her up on occasion. Jim Morrison overdosed on heroin that this dealer provided, fueling more vicious rumors as to her morality and the extent of her involvement in the death of the beloved Doors front man.

In 1972, John Dunbar began court proceedings to claim

custody of their son, Nicholas, although Dunbar also had a small, albeit manageable, drug problem. Eva Faithfull had been taking care of Nicholas while Marianne was off being a homeless drug addict. When the court granted Dunbar full custody, Eva overdosed on liquid morphine and survived. In *Faithfull*, Marianne recalled the effect her drug-taking had on her mother: "I honestly hadn't given a thought to what effect my behavior might have on her. That's the trouble with selfishness of this kind — the drug kind. The last thing you think about is 'how is this affecting my mother?'"[9]

Marianne spent the rest of the 1970s plunging headfirst into the abyss. It was a new decade and a new era of narcotics, disillusionment, and tragedy. The radical optimism of the hippie generation had disintegrated under the weight of consecutive rock star deaths and the Manson murders: "a judgment on us all."[10] Faithfull bore the physical weight of this, of the deaths, as well as the weight of her own mythology. Addicts are adept at finding reasons to use, and Marianne Faithfull had plenty of reasons.

Being an icon or a celebrity does not mean that you make money. This is something I've learned after years of interviewing musicians I consider famous but who still live paycheck to paycheck, without health insurance or a mortgage. When normal people are broke, they swallow their pride and work menial, soul-sucking, sometimes humiliating jobs. As my own addiction progressed, my jobs got worse and more degrading: from barista to warehouse worker, janitor, door-to-door vacuum salesman, and finally a hobo. In that vein, celebrities sometimes take gigs far below their caliber of talent in order to make a buck. Against her better judgment, Marianne accepted a role in Kenneth Anger's 1972 short film, *Lucifer Rising*, the film that inspired the $400 "Lucifer" jackets popular with poor outsider punks who aren't actually poor. She played Lilith, a blonde, blue-eyed demon gallivanting somberly around the desert. It was Anger's most expensive film because it involved a trip to Egypt. At this point, Marianne was a daily heroin user. Anger was aware that she was an addict, but he needed an actress and thought Marianne's celebrity would benefit the film.

> I said to Marianne Faithfull, don't bring any drugs because they'll execute you. So she hid her heroin in her makeup box underneath her face powder. I think she was powdering her face with heroin.[11]

She was high throughout filming, completely broke, and believed that dabbling in the occult, even as an actor and nonbeliever, cast a menacing influence over her already dire situation. I think her bad luck was probably more the drugs than a ridiculous occult collage created by a vampire-looking guy who unironically worshipped Anton LaVey. Although she made some minor film and television appearances in the 70s, her big film comeback was in Sofia Coppola's *Marie Antoinette* in 2006. Marianne returned to television in *Absolutely Fabulous*—one of my favorite shows of all time—but, of course, I didn't recognize her in the 1990s because I was sheltered and uncultured in a horrible suburb in Massachusetts. She played God and Anita Pallenberg played the devil. They reminisced about 60s culture and lamented Edina's vanity and extreme dieting techniques.

"IT'S ALL OVER NOW, BABY BLUE"

I travel often for work — I interview musicians — usually in Los Angeles because that's where most of them end up. I remember the first time I flew home to Massachusetts after visiting a girlfriend. My phone rang as soon as my plane landed, and it was my girlfriend. "Just wanted to make sure you made it." I thought, this is why people partner up. Two weeks later, Donald Trump won the 2016 presidential election, and the girlfriend was incommunicado. I listened to "It's All Over Now, Baby Blue" gluttonously, but didn't recognize it as a premonition at the time.

> You must leave now, take what you need, you think will
>   last
> But whatever you wish to keep, you better grab it fast

Last year, I saw the girlfriend's photo in the *New York Times* wedding announcements (I read them because they're hilarious) with a woman I thought was a friend. Premonitions should always be taken very, very seriously—unless you're on heroin, making a Kenneth Anger film. But any other time, absolutely.

Faithfull recorded an updated version in 2018. A slower, stripped-down version of the classic, made more pertinent with the passing of time and in the midst of a shift toward a global anti-humanitarianism disguised as economic conservatism. She delivers the lines with a quiet deliberateness, resigned but hopeful. An idealistic tale of impending war and presumed consequences.

The vagabond who's rapping at your door
Is standing in the clothes that you once wore
Strike another match, go start anew
And it's all over now, Baby Blue

"It's All Over Now, Baby Blue" is the last track on Bob Dylan's 1965 *Bringing It All Back Home*—universally declared one of the greatest rock 'n' roll albums of all time. Marianne Faithfull's original version was recorded in 1971 but released on her album *Rich Kid Blues* in 1985. It's an up-tempo, straightforward rock interpretation of the apocalyptic folk classic and a bit of a bridge signifying the transition from her 60s voice to the far more emotive, honey-soaked growl that would come to define her. Her recording in 1971 also held a premonitory significance, forewarning both the cultural and political backlash that erupted out of the Swinging Sixties and her need to let go of the past old associations and start fresh. "Take what you have gathered from coincidence" could easily refer to her meeting the Rolling Stones and Andrew Loog Oldham — a meeting that kick-started her career in music and that happened completely by chance. Marianne expertly embodies the prophetic narrator warning of impending destruction, but her 70s rendition exhibits resignation rather than hope, and she did resign herself to the myths that had grown around her in the press and to the romantic image of the put-upon, drug-addicted genius.

II

FALLING FROM GRACE

TRAUMA IS A GATEWAY DRUG

In my non-expert opinion, trauma is the gateway drug to substance abuse. Marianne Faithfull, I assume, possesses a great deal of internalized trauma that likely informs her art and was also the catalyst for her rampant heroin addiction. At the risk of sounding melodramatic, I do wonder if it is possible to be born female and not experience trauma. Sure, there are varying levels of trauma — a smorgasbord of horrors — but an objectively minor traumatic event could have major psychological consequences on one person and roll off the shoulders of another.

I think the base trauma that all women live with is the sense of being on high alert at all times — and I do mean at all times: walking, jogging in public, in a classroom, in a hospital, in a shopping mall, at work, while applying for jobs, going out alone, walking in a parking garage, at a concert, at a sporting event, while traveling, while using public transportation, shopping, attending conferences, at church, at the gym, in the woods, on a boat, playing in bands, in the recording studio, at the beach, at the pool, while wearing clothes or not wearing clothes, going to the bathroom, living alone, doing anything alone, doing anything alone after dark. You get the idea. Life is a constant state of fight or flight, shoulders up, mild tension headaches, keys between your fingers, and off you go.

So, we're thrust into this life at birth — if you're lucky, your mother was expecting you and/or is glad you've been born — and into a world of incessant, vibratory misogyny. We are then culturally conditioned to adjust and react to a dominant heteropatriarchal culture that ebbs and flows in its subtlety, but has always been and continues to be violently sexist.

For Marianne Faithfull, beauty was an additional trauma in the mutating cultural context of the 60s in which men took advantage of and profited from her looks. Would traditional beauty be as traumatic in a global matriarchy? May we someday know the answer to this very important question. I don't think women need to be exceptional beauties in order to be manipulated or taken advantage of, and in this post-gender time, viewing beauty or femininity as tools of male oppression is perhaps an anachronistic argument altogether. However, I do think it is safe to say that women move about in the world conscious of their physicality, their femininity or lack of it, and with a sense that beauty and femininity affords them certain collateral or leverage. Although Marianne didn't realize she was beautiful until she saw herself on a movie screen for the first time, playing Ophelia in *Hamlet*, she knew that men found her attractive.

Oh, I knew I was nice-looking, but I didn't know I was *that* pretty. I didn't realise until I watched *Hamlet* in the 1970s [she played Ophelia to Nicol Williamson's prince]. I burst into tears when I saw myself. I thought, "Blimey — that's what I look like."[1]

She was acutely aware of how her beauty and her gender lent themselves to her pop commodification and sexualization and later fueled vicious rumors in the media. At the same time, she used them as tools to find her way in an entertainment industry that was unwelcoming and did not take her seriously as an artist. What's interesting is that a woman who embodied trauma from the moment she was born weaponized that trauma in order to live and ultimately made an enormous impact on the history and culture that sought to destroy her. And that's what male-dominated rock culture does to women — it destroys them or renders them invisible and does not hold itself accountable for those destructions or omissions.

The word "trauma" is off-putting. I don't like it. It sounds whiny. It gets thrown around these days like the word "abuse," which has repurposed interpersonal conflict. But trauma is personal, it is subjective, and almost everyone has it. Your parent forgetting to pick you up from soccer practice could be the precursor to a cocaine addiction. It is less about the event itself and more about how we internalize and make sense of the event. I would assume that a healthy person would not resent their parent for such a minor infraction while a less adjusted kid would assume the worst. Enter the self-loathing and cut to fifteen years later as that kid snorts lines off a toilet bowl in a coffee shop. (I just made that up.)

There's this myth that trauma is larger than life—catastrophic even—and then you, hypothetically, get sober, start intense therapy, and learn that your simple childhood was a land mine and a catalyst for your descent into depression and addiction. Marianne Faithfull's alcoholic mother, absentee father, and foray into pop stardom were traumatic events. Everything that happened before full-blown heroin addiction—her teenage marriage and attempt to start a family, her relationship with Mick, her sexual exploits and experimentation with drugs—were coping mechanisms. They were ways of escaping trauma and existing in an industry, scene, and culture that didn't value her as an artist and an individual, which is traumatic in itself. Navigating the world, as a woman, necessitates constant vigilance.

There's another myth that trauma, mental illness, and addiction fuel the creative process, but Marianne Faithfull didn't do anything substantive until *Broken English*. She wasn't exactly sober then, but she was working on it. The pop stuff isn't what makes her a canonical music icon. It's the shit she did post-forty, post-heroin—*Strange Weather*, *Before the Poison*, *Negative Capability*, and Kurt Weill's *The Seven Deadly Sins*—when she stopped glorifying the myth of the addicted, suffering artist and began, well, making art.

I've taken to adorning my body with tattoos of inspiring women. They all possess talent and personal stories littered with struggle, tragedy, and/or addiction—Judy Garland, Marianne, Edith Piaf. I guess Dolly Parton is the one who has traveled the straight and narrow: no alcoholism, no drug problem, might be involved in a secret, decades-long lesbian romance, but that's only problematic to heterosexuals.

My family moved into an old house when I was twelve. I had my own room for the first time, and this privacy gave me the opportunity to experiment with new hobbies and bad habits. I got away with smoking cigarettes and drinking for so long because I looked like a child until I hit puberty—much, much later than my peers. All I wanted were boobs, my period, and to be a famous musician. Because I was such an anxiety-ridden late bloomer, I emulated women I perceived to be "living the dream" (rock stars, actresses, heroin addicts, authors, and artists), in order to speed up the maturation process.

I started smoking in the sixth grade, after I got my first electric guitar. In the 1990s, I bought packs of Marlboros from a vending machine at Bickford's Restaurant and smoked in the woods with friends. I chain-smoked from eighteen to thirty-one. I can't say it was Marianne Faithfull's fault directly, but my bad habits were very much informed by romanticizing the bad habits of women before me. Correlation is not causation, but it is something.[2]

In her second memoir, *Memories, Dreams and Reflec-*

tions, Marianne writes candidly about William S. Burroughs and the Beat mythology of heroin use: "I didn't just fall into the junkie life, I'd made a study of it. . . . Now I have people fantasizing about me with a needle in my arm, just as I fantasized about the junkie life from William Burroughs's book."[3] Maybe bad habits are just familial-like lines of influence. At fifteen, I had no idea who Marianne Faithfull was, but I recognized her image — the blonde 60s hipster chick I would pass by in *Rolling Stone* on my way to a Courtney Love article. Courtney Love smokes like a fucking chimney, and I would bet money that Marianne's chic, smoking image directly or indirectly influenced a young Courtney to embark on a life of unhealthy habits. And so, Marianne Faithfull and I were connected by cigarettes, through generations of smoking rock star women, before my musical knowledge had fully formed.

My music career, education, and alcoholism flourished after high school. I moved into an empty room in an apartment in Providence, Rhode Island, with a couple of friends. I covered a hole in the wall with a dresser, made shelves out of milk crates, and put an ashtray next to my bed. At the time, there was nothing more romantic to me than smoking, drinking, and listening to records in this wallpapered asthmatic coffin.

In the early 2000s, when I was in my early twenties, I fell in love with Marian Evelyn Faithfull. I preferred her *Broken English*, cigarette-ravaged, post-heroin voice. I still do. A weathered heel on cool snowy-blue gravel, aged and resolute. A cup of tea that burns when it goes down, perfect for a sensitive masochist. She remained a behind-the-scenes staple for me during my descent into addiction. I listened to Marianne Faithfull alone, over bottles of Jack Daniels and cigarettes, and read about her when I had access to the internet. I admired her exploits and her ability to survive her addiction, although, at the time, I had no intention of surviving my own.

Toward the end of my drinking, I had taken to interviewing myself on the front stoop of a friend's brownstone. At that point, I was homeless, unemployable, I had lost my license, and was basically jobless minus a few shifts a week at a creperie where I snorted coke in the bathroom and made smoothies because I never successfully mastered the art of flipping the crepe without destroying it. In a period of eight years, I had gone from a shy, virginal, agreeable, moderately talented young woman to an unhealthy, depressed, inconsiderate, whiskey-guzzling coke whore with a penchant for threesomes because I still couldn't admit that I was gay, even in a blackout.

By the time I turned twenty-six, I had had countless regrettable sexual experiences, had attempted suicide twice, had been fired from jobs selling vacuum cleaners door-to-door, cleaning toilets, and selling insurance. I had been "intervened" by my family and a licensed interventionist. I had puked into various receptacles, bags, toilets, and closets and had passed out in a variety of places. I had been arrested, ostracized by most of my friends and family, and had resorted to sleeping in cars, friends' houses, or outside. Addiction is basically just lowering the bar each time you hit a new low until you get sober or die. I remember the morning I woke up in a sitting position on a friend's couch with a senior Pomeranian named Shine licking blood and vomit off my face.

"This is fine." I thought.

All these insane things happened, or I initiated this insanity with my insatiable appetite for whiskey and cocaine at the expense of everyone in my radius. But the way it ended was quietly pathetic, like watching the last bit of air escape from a slowly deflating balloon. I was staying with this friend who lived in a nice apartment that I had slowly overtaken with trash bags of belongings. After a few months of squatting and not paying rent, I got my eviction notice: "Be gone by the time we get back from this road trip," or something to that effect. I was a drunk. My memory is unreliable.

I spent a few days snorting the last of my coke, drinking whiskey, and interviewing myself aloud. I imagined myself a put-upon, undiscovered genius whose addiction was part of the creative mind. When I ran out of drugs, money, friends, clothes, and options, I surrendered to an apparition of a pink woman who covered me in an invisible blanket of peace and warmth, and I checked myself into rehab.

In hindsight, I think I wanted someone to rescue me or to ask how I was doing—to not ignore the blatantly obvious fact that I was virtually immobile, suicidally depressed, and constantly intoxicated. But I surrounded myself with people who also drank and used drugs, and by the time I surpassed their substance intake, it was too late.

Now that I interview musicians for a living, I find it funny that I thought some amount of celebrity or success would alleviate my addiction; how I fantasized about strangers caring about what I thought. At the time, I lacked a firm sense of self and had no solid identity outside of the music I listened to, the books I read, and alcohol. I mean, I was known as a chain-smoking whiskey drinker, and I wore it like a badge of honor. I thought it was mysterious.

I thought about Marianne Faithfull a lot when I was hanging on my stoop. She refers to living on a wall in Soho for most of the 70s. I had to Google "wall" because I thought maybe it was British slang for what we in the United States call a shooting gallery or flophouse. After further investigation, I discovered that the "wall" was in fact a literal wall, the remains of a bombed-out building inhabited by addicts. She describes herself at that time as constantly high and dissociative, unable to differentiate between herself and what people had made her, and seeking out hard times in an attempt to be a Great Artist. She needed privacy and time to think, really. Her career was over by twenty-five, and she was washed-up, a has-been before thirty. She partnered with men who used her for her celebrity but were ashamed to be associated with her—that's how far she had fallen from the 1960s pedestal. So, she succumbed to anorexia, shot heroin religiously, lived on the wall, and waited to die or disappear, which is a pretty universal story when it comes to addicts. Francis Bacon, the painter, would stop by periodically and take her to lunch, which is not so common.

She was single for most of 1971 and 1972, living between the wall and her mother's house, until she met Oliver Musker. Why men enter into a relationship with an active heroin addict, even if she is Marianne Faithfull, is beyond me, but Marianne credits Oliver with saving her life. A temperamental aristocrat and antiques dealer, he was working as a shop assistant when the two met. He encouraged Marianne to get inpatient treatment and visited her at the facility several times a week with her mother, Eva, whose company he enjoyed.

Marianne had left her pop career entirely, or it left her in its corporate dust. She hoped to revisit her acting career, but her reputation preceded her, and it was nearly impossible for her to find a job. The couple befriended Angie and David Bowie after Bowie invited Marianne to perform in his *1980 Floor Show* in 1974. They sang "I Got You Babe" — Marianne wore a nun's habit — and she did a version of Noel Coward's "20th Century Blues." She tried to give David a blow job during a party, but he was too terrified of Oliver to accept the offer.[4]

Marianne was a has-been in the music scene at this point and a bit of an embarrassment to her former friends and acquaintances — except for Keith Richards and Anita Pallenberg, who saw Oliver as her great escape, her knight in shining armor. Her relationship with Oliver certainly cleaned her up, but her feelings for him began and ended with the debt she felt she owed him. He was codependent and needed her constant attention and she was a reader and a dreamer. Ultimately, it was a relationship of convenience. She and Musker parted ways amicably, and she gradually returned to drug taking.[5]

The improbability of her ever getting an acting gig drew Faithfull back to the music business. Her return was impeded by her reputation, and, in the 1970s, she was all but formally exiled from London and settled in Ireland, where she was welcomed with open arms. In a stroke of luck, Marianne's former manager Tony Calder had been appointed CEO at NEMS Records and she finally got a record deal. They released *Dreamin' My Dreams* in 1976 to a lukewarm global reception. In Ireland, however, the title track entered the charts at number four and spent eight weeks in the *Irish Top 20*. She describes the album as spurious and forgettable in *Faithfull*, but credits its success in Ireland to the country's forgiving people. Her motives for making an English country album, or any album at all at that time, were to get back in the public eye, to do something a little different, but mainly to regain her footing as a performer and make money because she was constantly broke. The success of *Dreamin' My Dreams* in Ireland gave her the opportunity to record a follow-up album.

She married her second husband, punk musician Ben Brierly, in 1979. They met when Marianne convinced him to play in her touring band, and soon after she was living in his flat. They survived on her 100-pound per week record label allowance and most of that was spent on drugs. It is important to note how unsurprising this is: When addicts are given money, they spend it on drugs, despite their best intentions. Ben was Marianne's most passionate and volatile relationship. He was a major influence on *Broken English*, released in 1979, and is credited as the sole writer of the song "Brain Drain." The success of *Broken English* placed an irreparable strain on the relationship: "It's difficult if one of you is bigger than the other. . . . Ben came to perceive me as an oppressor who had more money, more power and more control than he did."[6] She spent all of the royalties from *Broken English* on heroin and designer clothes as her marriage disintegrated.

A PUNK COMEBACK

Punk provided a beneficial cultural context for Marianne's comeback in 1979 with *Broken English*. The punk scene was purportedly welcoming and inviting to women, despite the recorded history of the movement that remains largely male-centric.[1] This comeback coincided with the commercialization of punk. Under the management of Malcolm McLaren, the Sex Pistols inspired fans and followers in London like Siouxsie Sioux, Billy Idol, Joe Strummer, and members of the Slits. Their ensuing global notoriety prompted mainstream radio and audiences to catapult bands like the Clash to stardom. In 1976, a year before the punk explosion, Faithfull recorded *Dreamin' My Dreams*, which failed to revitalize her career.

Broken English proved the only way she could redeem herself. Her voice had changed drastically as a result of prolonged drug use, so in a way it was like the universe, or God, or whoever, had thrust its hand down her throat and forbade her from returning to pop, folk, country, or anything comfortable. *Broken English* was undoubtedly influenced both by Ben Brierly and by a changing culture —

er, explosion — that wiped away any remnants of the free-floating Swinging Sixties.

I think it's safe to say that punk as a genre and a scene is more forgiving than rock, but the egalitarianism and diversity of the punk movement has been subject to revisionist history. Punk history has been determined by definitions of style, musicianship (or non-musicianship), and oddly specific definitions of what is or is not punk, despite punk itself being somewhat indescribable. Yes, *Broken English* was considered a punk record although it is left out of explicitly punk histories, but the reasons it was considered punk are worth unpacking. Lyrically, it is explicit, and who doesn't want to hear Marianne Faithfull sing about getting her snatch spit on?

Each track on *Broken English* is raw, emotive, relatable, alluringly autobiographical, and deals with pertinent social and political issues. Her cover of "The Ballad of Lucy Jordan" is a housewife's lamentation of suburban life — it's as if the *Girl on the Motorcycle* never got out of the 'burbs. "Guilt" addresses her upbringing and the omniscient sense of guilt that permeates Catholicism. The title track takes on the Cold War: "What are you fighting for?" she asks. "It's not my security." More than forty years later, her gruff yet melodic vocal style, delivery, and uncensored lyrics make this record a revolutionary moment that granted permission to women who followed in her footsteps to express themselves explicitly and without apology. She created a new blueprint that began with her recording of "Sister Morphine" in 1969 and reached full maturation on *Broken English* in 1979 as the complex, spirited, independent woman and the impression she left paved the way for peers and successors—women like Debbie Harry, Patti Smith, Annie Lennox, and Siouxsie Sioux. Mainstream rock in the 1990s was filled with nonconformist women like Shirley Manson, Liz Phair, and Courtney Love who disrupted existing archetypes through explicit language, confessional lyrics, and an aggressive and uncompromising stage presence that politicized personal experience the way *Broken English* politicized Faithfull's struggles.

"Why D'Ya Do It" is the most sexually explicit song on *Broken English*, and a graphic examination of jealousy. The lyrics were written by sociopolitical poet and activist Heathcote Williams and intended for Tina Turner, but Faithfull convinced him to give her the song instead. She and her band wrote and recorded a seven-minute, reggae-infused punk anthem strewn with snarling lines about infidelity, revenge, and various slang for genitalia.

> Why'd ya do it, she said, why'd you let her suck your
> cock?
> Oh, do me a favor, don't put me in the dark
> Why'd ya do it, she screamed, after all we've said
> Every time I see your dick, I see her cunt in my bed

Big, gray mother, I love you forever
With your barbed-wire pussy and your good and bad
    weather

Romantic love is a social construct, but the rush of oxytocin that comes with the honeymoon period is nice. I moved to a college town in the Northeast to finish my undergrad when I was in my early thirties. Despite my ambivalence, I created a dating site profile and chose a series of flattering, candid photos that I hoped would attract likeminded individuals. I linked my Spotify account and chose "Why D'Ya Do It" as my Tinder anthem. I did not receive any matches.

At the age of 37
she realized she'd never ride
through Paris in a sports car
with the warm wind in her hair

This is the third verse of "The Ballad of Lucy Jordan," the second single on *Broken English*. The song was written by renowned anarcho-hippie-turned-children's book author and illustrator, Shel Silverstein. He began his career as a self-taught cartoonist and writer whose work was published in *Sports Illustrated* and *Playboy Magazine*. Silverstein was also a prolific songwriter and wrote a number of songs that became hits for other artists, including Loretta Lynn, Johnny Cash, Waylon Jennings, Kris Kristofferson, and Dr. Hook & the Medicine Show who originally re-corded "The Ballad of Lucy Jordan." The song details the mental deterioration of a suburban housewife who, in a fit of desperation, climbs onto a roof and either kills herself or is enlightened—it's sort of a "pick your own adven-ture" deal. It is a feminist anthem, addressing the experi-ential trap of Cold War-era women that Betty Friedan so eloquently named "the feminine mystique." The song has aged well, appearing on the *Thelma and Louise* soundtrack in 1991 and continuing to represent the gendered "problem that has no name."[2]

At the age of thirty-seven, I realized I would never ride a horse across the semi-arid plains of New Mexico unless I put the trip on a credit card. Lucy Jordan was on to some-thing when she highlighted the otherwise unremarkable age of thirty-seven as an age capable of inciting an exis-tential crisis.

For me, it wasn't suburban life or its trappings—I live alone, I've never wanted children, I'm perpetually single and, statistically, will probably be single forever. Instead, it was the steady hum of hard work and accomplishment, of always needing to be making something, doing some-thing, being recognized for a job well done, that can mani-fest as a kind of personal prison much like Lucy Jordan's kids, house, and husband.

I had a very minor, below-the-surface, existential break-down when I turned thirty-seven. I realized I had never been on a vacation: Like, I had never picked a place I wanted to visit and gone there without needing to have a job that would validate spending the money. I honestly do not understand the concept of leisure, but I do believe it is something I should embrace in order to live life to its fullest and not die prematurely of stress-induced heart disease. I had a second crisis when I realized how much more economical it is to be partnered while vacationing. When all of my friends get married, and there's no one left, how will I travel? I could travel as a single person, but how will I document all of my adventures without using a selfie stick? Where does this nauseating need to document my every move come from?

I Googled Georgia O'Keefe incessantly for weeks while listening to "The Ballad of Lucy Jordan." Georgia O'Keefe lived in the fucking desert, alone, and painted. She climbed on a ladder up to the roof of her dirt house every morning to survey the land and pick her subject. She had also been with her husband for twenty years and suffered a couple of nervous breakdowns over his infidelities before she reached peak, New Mexico, Georgia O'Keefe-level zen. "Don't be so hard on yourself," I say to my shadow self. Or whatever.

I went on the vacation to New Mexico with my friend Alex. We visited some hot springs, hiked, stayed at a ranch — and we did ride horses across the semi-arid plains of Abiquiu at sunset with a whiskey-drinking rancher who loved Tarantino films. I don't think Lucy Jordan jumped off the roof. I think she climbed back into the house, filed for divorce, and started over again. There are too many potential beginnings to opt out entirely.

Grammy-nominated *Broken English* was "un-punk" in its production and distribution—a major label release that remains a bit dated in its use of every available contemporary production technique and synthesizer at the time. If punk is DIY, anti-corporate, anti-establishment, one can argue that this release is decidedly *not* punk, even if offset by the drug-addled *Saturday Night Live* performance that everyone worried would ruin Faithfull's career.[3]

I purchased the entire 1979–1980 season of *SNL*, under the impression that her performance was disastrous. I braced myself for the physical discomfort that accompanies watching someone you love humiliate herself in public. As a former alcoholic, I wondered if perhaps my barometer for disaster is a smidge off, but I didn't think it was so bad. Sure, she lost her voice, but she had just done a bunch of drugs in the greenroom, so I would say executing both performances to the best of her inebriated ability is a testament to her unparalleled talent. If she didn't have the baggage of being a junkie orchestrating a professional comeback, she could have gotten away with saying she had a cold, but her reputation preceded her, and I could almost sense the judgment from the studio audience, forty years later, on my couch. Witnessing what I consider to be a mediocre performance made me think about how disastrous performances or disastrous people have been defined in popular culture and what kinds of people are able to successfully redeem themselves and maintain their careers in the wake of one such catastrophic event.

As unromantic as it is, substance abuse, drug addiction, alcoholism—whatever you want to call it—underlies almost every shocking occurrence in the history of rock music. Maybe not Ashlee Simpson or Milli Vanilli's lip-synching tragedies, but I would file those under poorly timed technical difficulties. Ozzy Osbourne was famously arrested for urinating on the Alamo; GG Allin is known for covering himself and his audiences in shit; Keith Moon and John Bonham were famous for their drunken antics until each asphyxiated on his own vomit; and Jim Morrison took his dick out a lot, not because he was sober. And, finally, the ill-fated Rolling Stones Altamont concert in December 1969—where an audience member (high on meth) was murdered by an intoxicated Hell's Angel and several others died from drug-related issues—has come to signify the actual end of the peace and love generation and is viewed retrospectively as both a tragedy and a useful historical metaphor rather than as the utter fucking disaster it was. Marianne Faithfull was just really high during her *SNL* performances. No big deal.

Women are, of course, held to strict yet arbitrary standards, and while pissing on a national monument, eating feces, exposing yourself, or being otherwise belligerently high and drunk in public might have made the aforementioned men notorious, their actions did not threaten their careers. Marianne Faithfull, however, was a victim of this double standard throughout her life, even as she battled her drug addiction and even while promoting a so-called punk album in typical punk fashion.

By the time she recorded *Broken English*, she was still addicted to heroin but making a concerted effort. Now, in the face of all that adversity, all those poor choices, and her ongoing addiction, how disastrous is one fucking *Saturday Night Live* performance, really?

I watched the rest of the *SNL* season after Marianne's performance, and I didn't witness a single disaster until Bob Dylan's appearance. Wearing a windbreaker and permanent scowl, he performed three songs from his album *Slow Train Coming* — an album I like — with a band of jolly white men and some backup singers. His falsetto cracked and caved during "I Believe in You," and the only way I could fathom how he was commanding the audience was to remind myself that he had already been branded a legend by, like, 1966. I think the veneration of asshole, mediocre white men is the real disaster.

The only thing that would make *Broken English*, or Marianne Faithfull, more punk would be inclusion in punk histories. Punk rock is an attitude more than a style or genre. Much like radical queerness, punk is state of mind, a way of living without subscribing to the status quo. I refer to Judy Garland as the original punk singer, unironically: Watching her perform is like witnessing a lightning rod, a human conduit, who may as well be moshing as she thrusts her hands in the air or pulls her hair out. Had slam dancing existed, I truly believe that all the gays in the front row would have participated. *Broken English* was Marianne Faithfull's comeback, her first resurrection.

Dangerous Acquaintances, her 1981 follow-up, is considered a largely forgettable rock-centered album featuring singles written by Marianne and arranged by Brierly, Barry Reynolds, and Steve Winwood. Personally, I think the album is more pop than rock, and it's a very consistent album. Every song is solid, but nothing is spectacular. Her vocals are sometimes buried beneath a dated, 80s-era musical soundscape that seems almost sacrilegious. The problem was that the album tried to replicate the success of *Broken English*. This was her second album on Island Records, and there may have been pressure to outperform *Broken English*. *Dangerous Acquaintances* did chart in almost every country *Broken English* charted, but overall, Faithfull's success has eluded numerical value and industry accolades. She has certainly never experienced any real commercial success in the United States, and Americans tend to have an ethnocentric view of music and popular culture. Faithfull has had more "numerical success" in Europe and remains a national treasure in France and the United Kingdom. If a tree falls beyond the borders of the United States and Americans don't hear it, does it make a sound? Well, yeah.

In 1983, Faithfull was still under contract to Island Records and recorded *A Child's Adventure*. The opening track is a cover of "Times Square," written by Barry Reynolds:

If alcohol could take me there
I'd take a shot a minute
And be there by the hour

She embodies a lonely character set against the backdrop of New York City, contemplating her escape by way of alcohol or Jesus Christ. In a way, she self-actualized her way into recovery from heroin addiction through this song. It acted as a propeller pushing her into a new phase of life, similar to the way her recording of "It's All Over Now, Baby Blue" portended the dissolution of the 60s.

During the recording of *A Child's Adventure*, she had a brief affair with Reynolds, and Ben Brierly divorced her. She was thirty-seven and a daily heroin and cocaine user. When she toured, she hid her drug use from her bandmates and drank to excess instead—a more acceptable bad habit. Her friend, the artists' model and famous muse Henrietta Moraes, attempted to clean her up throughout the 70s. Marianne hired Henrietta as a kind of tour manager and babysitter and although Moraes was also an addict, she found that she was unable to keep Faithfull clean and functional. Marianne didn't start the long road to recovery until 1985 when a member of the Island Records A&R team visited her in New York to discuss plans for a forthcoming album, found her high, and living in squalor. The rep reported back to the label, which, in turn, organized her admittance to Hazelden Clinic, an in-patient drug and alcohol rehabilitation hospital. She was thirty-nine years old.

It's ironic that heroin became the drug of choice for so many 60s icons, a generation that prided itself on peace, love, and understanding and promoted the benefits of community. Heroin is a selfish, numbing, solitary drug, and it creates selfish, solitary people. Drinking and doing drugs is easy unless you're an addict, and the unfair advantage that non-addicts have is the ability to stop. If you're an addict or alcoholic, you don't know until it's too late. And there is no stranger, or more helpless, feeling than being an independent, creative, and hardworking woman who has lost control of her life.

III

THE CHANTEUSE

STRANGE WEATHER

In recovery, we refer to the messy parts of addiction as "war stories," and they play a much less significant role than more important things like how the fuck you stay sober. Faithfull's life, especially her life according to the press, had been nothing but a succession of these war stories dotted with periodic commercial successes. War stories are interesting, amusing, tragic, and unrealistic. They glamorize the sex and drugs aspect of rock 'n' roll. In reality, rock stars who gluttonously consume drugs and alcohol either get sober or they die prematurely. The ones who die prematurely are further lionized in the great halls of rock history, existing as idols and angels whose candles "burned out long before your legend ever did."[1] Ironically, an early death is good for posthumous careers—Patsy Cline, John Bonham, Keith Moon, Billie Holiday, Jimi Hendrix, Amy Winehouse, Kurt Cobain, and other members of the 27 Club have become dehumanized iconographic caricatures of themselves.

Marianne Faithfull gets labeled a "survivor" a lot, and she hates it. I have also been called that, and I can only speculate about Faithfull's disdain for the word based on my own experience. Struggle and addiction are corresponding forces that depend on each other. To be addicted to anything presupposes disorder, disaster, chaos, and an acute lack of the basic follow-through needed to maintain a variety of relationships, whether they be work, romantic, or casual in nature. Active addiction is marked by a persistent devolution of functionality: memory loss, blackouts, a lot of vomiting and/or waiting to vomit. As you traipse the road of progressive addiction, you might experience physical accidents, falls, car accidents, homelessness, and institutionalization; you might have run-ins with the law, be incarcerated, and if you weren't unemployable before these run-ins with the law, you certainly will be after the fact.

Marianne only appeared to have her shit together — to be the mythical "functioning addict" — because she was famous and always had someone around to help (or enable) her, from lecherous husbands and boyfriends, to her mother, to record executives who sent her to rehab because she owed them another *Broken English*. In a world that made more sense, she would have left the entertainment industry, which, by definition, is totally unconducive to sober life.

I honestly don't know how she did it. My first attempts at sobriety, on my own terms, were utter failures, and I never managed to achieve twenty-four hours substance-free until I forfeited myself to the state and let them lock me away. I was only able to maintain my sobriety by physically extricating myself from old associations and starting over in a seaside town where I knew absolutely no one. When I considered starting a band, my designated halfway house counselor responded, "Nothing good happens after 10 p.m." I still believe that, and I did put music on the backburner for another eight years or so, until I felt confident that I wouldn't slip up. However, recovery is different for everyone and being dogmatic about it is counterproductive. I have always maintained this position, even while I was neck-deep in a recovery community.

Faithfull's recovery is difficult to pinpoint, and to define, because she's not a natural glutton — she's a practiced hedonist who had willingly committed herself to a Dionysian way of life. She experienced a lot of false starts in sobriety. Her drug of choice, as we say in the AA biz, is heroin. That was her Achilles heel. She did continue to drink socially after she kicked heroin and during a long romantic relationship with a "normal" (how we in the AA biz refer to those who can drink like normal people). This guy was successful and regimented but, like Marianne, enjoyed parties and the finer things in life. As far as I can gather, she eventually gave up drinking as well and is presently substance-free. In closing, I think sobriety is personal. It is not homogenous, and it can't be measured in relation to other people because although we are not unique, we sort of are.

There are class-, gender-, and race-based reasons why Faithfull was able to overcome her affliction, which counters the whole survivor myth. First of all, she didn't grow up considering the possibility of ever becoming a homeless drug addict. Statistically speaking, if you grow up around addicts, or you grow up poor or abused, you're likely to become an addicted adult. No, she wasn't rich, but she was privileged in other ways. She lived with an alcoholic parent, but it was the private, insular kind of alcoholism that middle-class life affords. When she spiraled into uncontrollable heroin addiction, her family was shocked. It was unexpected because she had *potential*. Larger culture has shown, time and time again, that addicts who are, for example, single black mothers, are not regarded as having the intrinsic potential of a single, white mother like Marianne Faithfull. Her cultured, bohemian upbringing completely contradicted what she became: a homeless heroin addict. And she always had the sense that to be an addict was unacceptable — it was a complete and total divergence from what was expected of her. Society doesn't expect anything from its throwaways. The reasons that Marianne drank and drugged were due to these internalized pressures and expectations — her marriage, her beauty, her irrelevance in an industry whose acceptance she craved — that she unsuccessfully sought to relieve in her relentless pursuit of hedonism. Ironically, her beauty, fame, and her mythology were the reasons she was given so many chances to get well.

In 2007, I admitted myself to a drug and alcohol rehabilitation program. One surprising thing about rehab is that they confiscate books and music that are not "recovery-based." I was prepared for the strip searches, the sleepless nights on a cot in a room with other detoxing women, the toiletries and razors that had to be returned after showering, the barred windows and no exercise. But I was not prepared to give up my music. I was admitted to the facility as homeless, which meant I was awarded, free of charge, a coveted state bed, extended stay, and weekly visitation privileges in a small, windowless room. Most of the other women had visitors who smuggled in makeup or drugs, but I insisted on burned compact discs that I would shove down my pants before exiting the visitation room. There were certain things my family wouldn't provide — anything too "depressing" ("No Cat Power!") and no Judy Garland because she was both depressing and an alcoholic. An acquaintance visited once — I think he was curious about the place. He wrote vacuous short stories about the trials and tribulations of white, college-educated, red-headed young men, and he was a redhead and a Brown University graduate. He brought me a Marianne Faithfull mix, and I never saw him again.

I needed a creative outlet while I was getting sober, but I associated all those outlets with drinking and drugging. My guitar sat in the corner of whatever sober house room I was renting, gathering dust, because I couldn't bear to touch it. It made me physically sick. When I did try to write a song, I couldn't escape the limitations of my current life, which consisted of AA meetings and sobriety. I worried that I had become a kind of one-dimensional character, that living sober meant being uninteresting. Most of my rehab friends listened to mainstream pop and rap music. They wore Victoria's Secret sweat suits, smoked cigarettes, and went to concerts together, pounding Redbull and preaching the gospel of sober living. I appreciated their enthusiasm but felt lost, bored, and uninspired. I listened to Marianne Faithfull and mourned my former misery because at least I found joy in the music and had something interesting to say about it. She was precious to me — a relic of my past that I didn't want to leave there. When I got sober, I had to get to know her again, in a new way, so as not to lose myself in that association. It is really fucking easy to feel sorry for yourself. It is, I imagine, even easier to pick up a drink or a drug, but I've managed to avoid that so far.

At four years sober, I was invited to perform a benefit show in Providence, Rhode Island, and my return to live music came by way of Madonna covers. I went back to school and slowly incorporated old hobbies and interests into my busy schedule. I covered Marianne Faithfull songs, mostly different renditions of "It's All Over Now, Baby Blue," which I have always considered to be more her song than Bob Dylan's. I slowly and deliberately willed my own creative juices to flow through identification, and eventually it worked.

The 1987 *Strange Weather* is Marianne Faithfull's first sober studio recording after barely surviving a seventeen-year heroin addiction. She had attempted suicide, overdosed countless times, saw the specter of death twice, lost her front teeth, broken her jaw while under the influence and had it wired shut, been hospitalized, and lost her relationship with her son. But it was the death of a manic-depressive schizophrenic that wrenched her life into focus. In recovery, it is suggested that newcomers refrain from entering into romantic relationships or pursuing any major changes for the first year of sobriety. I would say the vast majority ignore this important unwritten rule and wholeheartedly embark upon the "13th step," which is how we jokingly refer to new AA couples. Marianne met Howard Tose (Howie) when they were patients at Hazelden. She was a garden-variety drug addict, emotionally immature with unresolved trauma. Howie, though, was "dually-diagnosed": a manic-depressive schizophrenic with multiple addictions to hard drugs. After graduating from Hazelden, they lived together in Boston, played house, and tried to get sober until Marianne realized how sick he actually was. She sat him down and explained everything. His last words before jumping to his death from their thirty-sixth floor bedroom window were, "The honeymoon's over then, huh?"[2]

Marianne got clean, for good, after Howie's death. She moved into a new apartment in Boston with her mother, Eva, who was still a functioning alcoholic, but Marianne started making better personal choices—like not going into the liquor store to buy Eva's bottle. She was a zealous convert to the *Big Book of Alcoholics Anonymous*, worked the steps, got a sponsor, and experienced what is known in recovery as a "pink cloud." I never experienced the high of the pink cloud—a euphoric stage in early recovery—and so I never suffered the loss of being thrust out of its state of grace, but Marianne was eager and ecstatic about her recovery. Eva was proud of her daughter, but worried she was becoming too sober, a phenomenon that occurs when you clean up and the people around you keep drinking and drugging.[3]

Faithfull had her last shot of heroin in 1985. She had visited an oral surgeon about excruciating pain in her jaw—something she had let go far too long and passed off as the pain of straight living—and discovered that her jawbone was slowly rotting from an old break and a botched wisdom tooth removal. Because of her history with drugs, the doctor opted to wire her jaw shut rather than operate.

In 1986, she attended a Bob Dylan and Tom Petty and the Heartbreakers show in Boston. She noticed Bob eyeing her curiously after the performance with her jaw bolted shut, the metal handle sticking out of her face, and a new, positive outlook on life. She launched into her recovery story; he was unimpressed.

His reaction was fairly typical of the rock contingent. They liked me better on heroin. I was much more subdued and manageable. It's very common with rock stars. They surround themselves with beautiful and often brilliant women whom they also find threatening. One way out is for the women to get into drugs. That makes them compliant and easier to be with.[4]

Men need their muses, and they need them to be attractive, subservient, and pliable. Men as individuals are not solely responsible for this attitude. Blame it instead on male-dominated and male-curated media and history. Bob Dylan's less-than-enthusiastic reaction to Marianne Faithfull's sobriety; Mick Jagger's revulsion at her weight gain in 1972; Ben Brierly's resentment of her success with *Broken English*. It is a complete disservice to women, and in this case, to women in rock history, to relegate them to predetermined, supplementary categories and to condemn them for wanting or being more.

It is oddly comforting that addiction is indiscriminate in its consequences, regardless of gender, age, race, or whether you kill yourself by jumping out a window, overdosing in a subway station, passing out in the toilet, or living to readjust and tell the tale. All of the consequences become painful associations in sobriety. Marianne knew she was in too much pain to write, or maybe that composing original material was too dangerous, but she was determined to filter the devastation she was feeling about Howie's death, and she did so by interpreting classic jazz and blues love songs. Friend and curatorial genius, Hal Willner, was the person who took the time to sit around, listening to records with her as she fought for inspiration.

Strange Weather marks the end of Marianne Faithfull's pink cloud and readmittance into a life worth living on its own terms.

Strange Weather was a stepping-stone for Marianne Faithfull like the Madonna cover show was for me. In 1985, Willner recruited her for his project, *Lost in the Stars: The Music of Kurt Weill*. Tom Waits also contributed to the album, and when she and Hal decided to collaborate on a covers album, Marianne called Tom, who penned the title track with his wife, Kathleen Brennan.

> Will you take me across the channel
> London bridge is falling down
> Strange a woman tries to save
> What a man will try to drown

The record was a critical success, even heralded as her "second comeback," and she reinforced her new role as torch singer, chanteuse, and interpreter. Her ability to make the songs her own is a testament to her capacity to communicate them convincingly. This gift is no doubt a result of lived experience and her unique ability to identify with a wide range of subject matter.

In a 1988 album review, Chris Morris says, "Faithfull displays a virtuosity on *Strange Weather* that exists outside the music. The sound of a life that has been lived—the sound Faithfull displays on *Strange Weather*—is a rare, powerful, and beautiful one, and one that few singers of her gen-

eration can generate."[5] In the same interview, he notes
that novelist Terry Southern aptly compares Marianne to
Billie Holiday, Marlene Dietrich, and Lotte Lenya, whose
strengths went beyond technical ability and "lay in a kind
of extramusical quality of feeling and experience." Another
notable review said, "From Marianne Faithfull, music to
slit your wrists by," which is a pretty accurate description
of the album and of early sobriety.[6] She was forty years old
when she finally kicked heroin for good, and thank fucking God, because look at the catalogue of masterpieces we
would have missed out on. The best work of her life was
yet to come.

Marianne Faithfull is a songwriter, but she's also a chanteuse and an interpreter of songs. *Strange Weather* was
a way for her to ease back into songwriting safely without having to stoke the flame of addiction by delving too
deeply into her emotions, which were, very likely, volatile,
as they often are in early recovery. At this point in time,
interpreting standards, cover songs, and original composi-
tions written for her by other people was a way to eschew
the emotional toll of penning her own work.

At the same time, there is an assumption that "singers"
are not musicians and that interpretation is simply mimicry.
I've often fielded these kinds of comments when I've interviewed singers: "Does she write her own songs or just
sing?" The history of rock 'n' roll privileges virtuosity and
technical ability, and this opinion has become general con-

sensus. It is another gender-induced phenomenon rooted in decades of sexist media and historiography. There is a genius and a particular kind of artistry inherent in conveying other people's words with authority. Marianne Faithfull doesn't cover songs; she inhabits them and translates them in a way that makes them believably her own.

A life that overshadows an artist's work doesn't lessen the authenticity of the work or affect the ability to move an audience. In Marianne Faithfull's case, it strengthens her ability to write from a place that is universally known and understood by everyone who has faced challenges in their life. Her unique history strengthens her capabilities as an interpreter, making her able to revisit certain songs again and again with different results. Consequently, her talent for communicating across generation and genre is unparalleled. Her rendition of "As Tears Go By" on *Negative Capability* takes on an entirely different meaning in 2018 than it did in 1964.

Female musicians, Marianne Faithfull in this case, are predisposed to certain artistic conundrums: private lives that overshadow work; the burden of ever being crowned a celebrity, pop star, or girlfriend; the problem of being physically beautiful (or not beautiful enough). Then there is the unfortunate problem of image — that is, drug taking did not reflect on Marianne the same way it did on the Stones, the Beatles, or Bob Dylan. There were repercussions for her while male musicians, for the most part, enjoyed image enhancement. The same goes for the songs.

Faithfull has always had to justify her existence and her validity in the industry. Her ability to convey emotion through cover songs has been heralded a God-given gift in music media, but she has had to fight to be taken seriously as a songwriter. Her perseverance and constant demand for recognition in all facets of the creative process has helped dispel the myth that women's stories and perspectives are not universal.

THE '90S: A GOOD DECADE FOR WOMEN IN ROCK

The 1990s were a great decade for women in rock music. Hole, L7, Belly, the Breeders, PJ Harvey, Garbage, No Doubt, Luscious Jackson, Elastica, Portishead, Veruca Salt, and Throwing Muses somehow made their way into public consciousness while the underground Riot Grrrl movement found themselves deflecting media attention. All of a sudden, women were the harbingers of their own success, on their own terms. The existing female archetypes were complicated by swaths of red lipstick and feminist messages scrawled on bare midriffs in indelible marker. The honeymoon, however, lasted just under a decade. The first round of backlash emerged with a new wave of hyper-masculine male rock bands like Limp Bizkit and Korn and fully materialized with the disastrous Woodstock '99, with a legacy of violence against women perpetrated against a backdrop of this new wave of misogynistic male rock.

One month after Woodstock, Adam Horovitz of the all-male Beastie Boys accepted the MTV Video Music Award for Best Hip-Hop Video and, at the urging of his long-time partner Kathleen Hanna of Bikini Kill, addressed the assaults from the stage: "I read in the news and heard from my friends all about the sexual assaults and rapes that went down at Woodstock '99. And that made me feel really sad and angry. OK? Are you all there? OK." Festival promoter John Scher believed that the focus on the sexual assaults was an example of the liberal, disaster-oriented media, exaggerating what was actually a very minor issue. He used a theoretical yardstick to counter critics, saying that, yes, in fact, women were "exploited," but it wasn't like they were "getting raped every 15 feet." Whipping out the age-old justification, "Well, look at what she was wearing," Scher said, "I am critical of the hundreds of women that were walking around with no clothes on. You know? And expecting not to get touched."[1] So, basically, more women who attended Woodstock '99 were not sexually assaulted than were sexually assaulted, and how were men supposed to control themselves in what was essentially a field day for rapists? Sexual assault is paradigmatic of sexism in larger society. While the 90s brought a feminist wave and thoughtful male rock stars like Kurt Cobain and Eddie Vedder to the mainstream, Woodstock '99 removed the mask from a generation of young men who had supposedly been listening.

At the turn of the century, women in the music industry who had been chart-topping successes found themselves blacklisted from rock radio or syphoned off into women-centered stations. Sarah McLachlan initiated the women-centered traveling festival Lilith Fair in 1997, but it too was a victim of backlash and ended in 1999.[2] In the aftermath of the 9/11 terrorist attacks and the ensuing war on terror, the United States valiantly shifted to the earlier Cold War mythology of the protective male and dependent female. In her book, *The Terror Dream*, author Susan Faludi investigates the disappearance of women in the media—commentators, scholars, news anchors, and editorialists—but this disappearance extended to musicians, artists, and entertainers as well.[3] There was no room for rebellious, feminist women in the new and improved national security state. Further, the Cold War trend of fragile, heteronormative, femininity was used to repurpose and commodify the subversive messages of the Riot Grrrl movement—Bikini Kill's 1991 *Revolution Girl Style Now!*, for example—and turn them into something more acceptable and profitable, like the Spice Girls' Girl Power! slogan. The 2000s marked the rise of sexualized yet arguably autonomous female pop stars like Britney Spears and Christina Aguilera, and a series of nondescript boy bands like N'Sync and Backstreet Boys. By 2002, bands like Hole and Garbage were no more, and the national Riot Grrrl movement had all but dissolved.

Marianne Faithfull released five albums throughout the 1990s while in her mid-forties and early fifties. The progenitor of nonconformist "bad" women of rock, she eschewed the fallout experienced by a younger generation of heavily publicized rocker women, carving out a space for herself in the annals of mainstream celebrity. Faithfull had aged out of popular relevance and embarked on a kind of cabaret crooner journey. I'm a big fan of vocalists. Old-timey singers. This is what I listen to at home, but it doesn't exactly flip the script, stylistically, for women to sing jazz and blues covers once they've aged out of perceived relevance.

Faithfull's choice, however, was partially aimed at pleasing her parents. When she covered Kurt Weill's *The Seven Deadly Sins* in 1998, for instance, it was a tribute to her father, Glynn. Life on life's terms is not as interesting as life on heroin for biographers and journalists, but it is a lot more productive. Mark Hodkinson spends just as much time documenting her post-degenerate rock star days as he does on her early life and career. But sober life, more often than not, consists of quietly rebuilding. It is the antithesis of drug-taking and destroying everything in your wake. Marianne stayed clean through a divorce and the deaths of both her parents, and she curated a new image out of the rubble of her past. She toured consistently while battling periodic health issues. Being high all the time masks the fact that your body is deteriorating rapidly, and when you get sober, everything hurts. Glynn Faithfull died in 1996 while Marianne was in rehearsals for the live recording of *The Seven Deadly Sins*. The two had made amends after she published her first biography in 1994. Marianne sent her father a copy, and he sent her a letter in return that precipitated a new closeness in his dying days. She details her mother's death in 1990 and describes a deep love and admiration for her: "My mother was the first manifestation of the Great Goddess." They found a resolution that they hadn't seemed capable of achieving in life.

It was relieving to read, especially as a fellow addict who knows the dangers of resentment, but also as a grown woman navigating a rather fraught relationship with my own mother. Isn't everyone though, in some way? It's the defining relationship in all our lives. The patriarchy and all of its manifestations (religion, the father) are sad attempts to disempower the divine mother, the goddess, the divine feminine. All of it. Marianne spent much of the 1990s working to become a respectable artist by channeling Kurt Weill and performing *The Seven Deadly Sins*, which had become something of a second career. Weill's music corresponded to her own moodiness and was a way of connecting to her mother and to Eva's world.[4] This emotional and artistic connection produced three Weill-inspired recordings and performances, and by the end of the decade, she felt she had explored the extent of the canon to the best of her ability, vowing to change musical direction.

In the midst of perfecting her cabaret style, she released two albums of original material: *A Secret Life*, produced by Angelo Badalamenti in 1995, and *Vagabond Ways* in 1999. *A Secret Life*, a popular rock album inspired by Faithfull's interest in classical music, was released to mixed reviews. *Vagabond Ways* was more straightforward rock. Produced by famed rock engineer Daniel Lanois, it was a bit like a bridge to the more contemporary, pop/rock style of the 2002 *Kissin' Time*.

Discernment is an art, and Faithfull is a master at creating and cultivating relationships with musicians and artists who serve her songs well. For someone who prefers Frank Sinatra, Sarah Vaughn, and Weill to contemporary music, she has remained attuned to high-brow rock culture since the 1990s. Biographers and critics focus on the obvious Jagger/Richards collaboration and her personal and professional (sometimes both) relationships with various men in her life. But Faithfull has had long-standing musical partnerships with Nick Cave and Warren Ellis, Barry Reynolds, and Hal Willner. Roger Waters and Steve Earle have written songs for her. Her relationship with Reynolds, which began with *Broken English*, produced the song "Times Square," my favorite song about New York, and the only thing I like about the city presently. Listening to Marianne sing that song on the Hollywood Bowl recording is transformative.[5] She cloaks the memory of a desolate, punk rock, crime-ridden New York of the 1970s and 80s in a husky sentimentality without a hint of regret — something only she and that voice can accomplish. Barry Reynolds forfeited his right to ever sing it again once he handed it over to her. All these collaborations, objectively speaking, have had more of an impact on her career, and have produced more music, than the five or so years she spent in the orbit of the Rolling Stones.

I play drums in a drag-infused punk band called Feminine Aggression with two friends. It's taken me thirty-eight years to refer to myself as a musician even though I have played instruments and made music for most of my life. I had absorbed a lifetime of insults, criticism, and backhanded compliments and determined that I lacked the skill, knowledge, and expertise required to personally identify as a musician. Although I would sometimes admit to "kind of" playing guitar, I never called myself a drummer. It was such a carefully guarded secret that a close friend messaged me on Facebook asking why I had never told her I was a musician.

When I moved to western Massachusetts, I started volunteering at a local arts collective and subsequently attended more shows. I noticed that cis men didn't seem to be ashamed of their lack of musical ability; they're all armed with an implicit confidence whether or not they (or their band) suck. Finally, at thirty-seven, I decided to be the meme I wanted to see in the world—the one that says, "go forth with the confidence of a mediocre white man," or something to that effect. I began referring to myself as a drummer. I proudly promoted our band. I wore jumpsuits, crowd surfed, and danced without reservation. It's liberating—more so for someone approaching middle age at a time when *Glamour* magazine tells me I should cut my hair into a sensible bob and start draping myself in linen.

I do resent the Western notion that feminist liberation requires some amount of nudity. I wear sweatpants and socks to bed and feel completely freed from the confines of reality every single night. That being said, it is liberating to have options, to not feel as though you are condemning people to a traumatic injury by breastfeeding in public or, you know, stripping down to a bra to pound a drum set. In 1999, Marianne posed for a series of photographs by David Bailey dressed in sheer black tights, a black lace bra and underwear, and black wristband. She was fifty-three years old and looked her age — such a refreshing sight. Whatever their intent was, Bailey and Faithfull created a series that juxtaposed these photographs with saucy shots taken by Terry O'Neill in the early 1960s that were meant to transform her convent school image and re-brand her a sophisticated sex kitten. The most noticeable thing about both sets of photographs is how much more at ease Marianne looked, posing in her underwear, in her fifties than she did in her twenties. This is my archetype.

BEFORE THE POISON

François Ravard was born in 1957, when Marianne was eleven. A French music and film producer, he is the brains and the brawn behind the enormously successful French all-male rock band, Telephone, and he has contemporized Faithfull's recordings since the mid-1990s. Ravard is a ghost-like free agent whose resume is peppered with the occasional traditional job. The quintessential alchemist and producer, a man who knows everyone, he has virtually no internet footprint, making magic behind the scenes. He founded his own production company in 1987 and produced a number of shorts and three feature films — most notably, the 1990 *Stan The Flasher*, directed by Serge Gainsbourg. Ravard was introduced to Marianne Faithfull by journalist Philippe Constantin in 1994 and quickly became her manager, producer, and romantic partner, encouraging her to expand her collaborations and to extend her efforts in fields beyond the music industry — theater, cinema, live recordings, and world tours. He got her cast as Pegleg in *The Black Rider: The Casting of the Magic Bullets*, an avant-garde musical fable based on a book by William S. Burroughs and created by theater director Robert Wilson and musician Tom Waits. Ravard worked with her on *20th Century Blues* in 1997 and organized her world tour in support of the album. Perhaps more importantly, he initiated her post-Weill transition into contemporary rock with *Vagabond Ways* in 1999 and *Kissin' Time* in 2002.

Faithfull was (maybe still is?) a big Smashing Pumpkins fan and met Billy Corgan backstage after a Pumpkins gig. He liked Marianne so much that he offered to work with her on her next album, whenever she wanted, and free of charge, in one of the only stories I've ever heard about Billy Corgan that doesn't make me want to punch him in the face. Ravard also involved Beck, Damon Albarn of Blur, and Jarvis Cocker in her recordings. He has a lot of contacts and these are especially useful in his home country. In France, unlike in the United States and Britain, an aging female torch singer remains a valued institution, and Faithfull has experienced more commercial success abroad than in the United States.

In my humble, unpopular opinion, Faithfull struck gold with *Before the Poison* in 2005. This is the record on which her younger collaborators coaxed the epochal poetic rock-cabaret hybrid style that has come to define her catalogue to the present. I imagine the recording studio like a middle school lunchroom. Marianne is at the head of the cool kids' table because she is the queen, and her chosen followers are the hip, Goth, art, stoner kids who all probably had sex when they were twelve and carry cigarettes in their backpacks: Nick Cave and his Bad Seeds, PJ Harvey, Mark Lanegan, and Damon Albarn.

A recurring theme in the Marianne Faithfull song catalogue is the tension between a life of quiet domesticity and her unshakeable status as an icon. She has removed herself from relationships that subdued her creative spark and entered into others hoping to build something long-lasting with men who were unable to separate the myth from the woman. It is easy to place her lived experience in the lyrics.

Before the Poison includes several songs by PJ Harvey. She wrote the music to "Mystery of Love," a song about love's elusive nature:

> When you're not by my side
> The world's in two, and I'm a fool
> When you're not in my sight
> Then everything, just fades from view

Harvey also wrote the music for the Kinks-esque '90s rock anthem "My Friends Have," which is quite simply about the importance of friendship:

> My friends have always been there
> To help me shape my crooked features
> My friends have picked me up again
> And pushed my enemies out of the picture

Marianne Faithfull might be the only singer able to deliver the phrase "I love these friends of mine" in all earnestness and be taken seriously. I love that song and I hate earnestness. Critics misunderstand lyrics like "Tell me, do we still have time? To make the wrong somehow be right?" from the record's title track. And I guess the words are sad if you think about them in the context of romantic love as the brass ring in the merry-go-round of life, but I find them empowering. Reviewers have constantly shortchanged her by ghettoizing her as the sad, lovelorn survivor and the deliverer of everlasting bad news.

Faithfull dismisses her relationship with the Stones, with Mick in particular, as fortuitous yet largely inconsequential in the grand scheme of things. She's polite but sarcastic when she talks about him. She has a piece of Rolling Stones memorabilia displayed in her bathroom . . . in front of the toilet. If I were her, I would be resentful and dismissive, too, because her professional history is all tangled up in his when she has outproduced and surpassed him creatively for fifty years. She was a kid when they were together. But they were also together during a transformative time in her life: from married pop star and mother to girlfriend, drug addict, and media fodder. She attempted suicide at the end of their relationship and became a heroin addict, which is just a slower, more tedious death. When it finally ended, she simply gave up. There were more relationships after that, of course, but Mick is the one who emerges over and over again in every autobiography. He might not be the love of her life — I hope he isn't because he's an asshole — but he is a defining relationship.

The song "Desperanto" was co-written by Nick Cave and performed by the Bad Seeds. "Desperanto" is a black pun on Esperanto, the universal language created in 1887 by L. L. Zamenhof. Faithfull's "Desperanto" is a language of the despair that results from allowing another person to absorb you.[1] The obsession, repetition, and disconsolate self-flagellation that is so often mistaken for love. A chorus of men repeat the phrase, "Everybody loves my baby / Everybody loves my baby / Everybody loves my baby now."

It sounds like the Rolling Stones' "Sympathy for the Devil," a song about the devil, told from his point of view, a "man of wealth and taste." And I guess after all this time, Marianne still has sympathy for the devil.

Music criticism existed in some form or another before the 1960s, but the Beatles made it a prominent and lucrative endeavor for men writing about popular music. Rock criticism today exists in the vast expanse of the internet and consists of established critics and amateurs. From its beginnings, the "ideology of rock criticism" has been to summarize and simplify. It valorizes serious, masculine "authentic" rock and dismisses trivial, feminine "prefabricated" music, which it eventually moved into its own category: Pop.[2] This has been the gendered framework within which critics have shared and validated their opinions, resulting in a male-dominated field that defines taste and determines an artist's access to audience.

Drug-addicted, gun-toting Hunter S. Thompson introduced a new genre with gonzo journalism, which didn't pretend to be objective, and Lester Bangs wrote about music in a signature first-person, free-form, and deliberately insulting manner. He has since been anointed "America's Greatest Rock Critic" for what amounts to jerking himself off while simultaneously patting himself on the back for a job well done. Engaging in rock criticism often requires that women refer to a set of standards and employ male-appointed cultural references that might not be their references. They are encouraged to be objective, to refrain from naval-gazing, to subsume their voices beneath the cold veneer of fact, knowing full well that the "facts" were written by men. So how can they forge a different path, like gonzo journalism, or make a meaningful dent in the field when it was designed to maintain the status quo?

I can't take rock critics seriously because they pretty much get paid to lie — and there are levels of lying, from little white fibs to pathological lies. Rock criticism is harmless on its own, but chronically dangerous as an institution, legitimate only in its history and perceived relevance. The problem with rock critics is that they don't actually know what they're talking about and they're too proud to admit it. As a field, it is a collection of emotional projections. The fact that some projections are more valuable than others is absurd. And none of this means that I don't enjoy music writing, because I do, very much. But I resent the preciousness, the sexism, and the gatekeeping aspect of what is, essentially, a field of opinion masquerading as expertise.

Ninety percent of Marianne Faithfull's reviews were written by men and follow a pattern over time. First, she was pretty and polite, as evidenced in Peter Jones's feature, "Marianne Faithfull Is a 'Real' Nice Person," in the *Record Mirror* in 1964. New fans learned that the seventeen-year-old blonde, "a sweetie, a doll, a dish," had the ability to make men's heads swivel approvingly.[3] A few years later, she was the slutty "Girl in the Rug," a Rolling Stones groupie,[4] and a mediocre actress (but pretty). Then she was a pretty, drugged-out failure in the 1970s, who had released a flop; a phoenix rising from the ashes of the 1960s with *Broken English*; and finally, a legend, not immune to criticism or commercial flops, but safe from insult in her well-earned bubble of respect.[5]

It's important to expand the collective field of criticism because, in Marianne Faithfull's case, it proposes a very limited view of a multifaceted artist. If you were, for instance, asked to read the existing collection of male-dominated reviews and write a summary of her musical career, it would be an unmoving portrait of a legendary sad woman who writes sad songs, forever teetering on the precipice of extinction. What critics haven't adequately documented is her humor, her propensity for absurdity—how being born female is a political act and surviving is contingent on embracing the absurd. But I suppose if you're not born into battle, all of that can sound a bit depressing.

I never listened to *Dangerous Acquaintances*, her 1981 follow-up to *Broken English*, until I started working on this book. It is widely documented as a forgettable throwaway that epically failed to come close to the success of its predecessor. Mark Millan gave it one line in the *Daily Vault*: "She unfortunately let her guard down rather quickly with the flat, uninspired follow-up, *Dangerous Acquaintances*."[6] Imagine my surprise when I sat down, played the album, and enjoyed it! No, it's not a life-affirming document. It doesn't transcend time and space, but it is a consistently decent rock album.

Her 2005 album *Before the Poison* is another personal favorite. Although it didn't receive nearly as many tepid reviews, many reviewers seemed determined that she never emotionally evolve. A review in *Pitchfork* claimed that "Marianne Faithfull has one singing tone: grim. Her Gothic voice conveys gravity perhaps better than any other rock-oriented singer alive, but that ability comes with its own limitations: While Faithfull can make grim sound bitter, biting, resigned, or determined, she can't make it sound triumphant or joyful."[7] But a voice cannot be Gothic or convey anything on its own. Marianne Faithfull has smoked a lot of cigarettes. Reviewers project their personal feelings regarding the cumulative events of her life that contribute to her legend onto something as benign as a voice irrevocably changed by nicotine. They claim to be objective, but they are partial to existing female archetypes and unable to be impartial beyond those margins.

I found *Before the Poison* to be introspective and, at moments, victorious. "The Last Song," co-written with Blur front man Damon Albarn, is a perfect example of Faithfull's ability to procure victory from something so sonically despondent. Made up predominantly of minor chords, "The Last Song" deals with loss — perhaps a literal loss of home due to gentrification or the loss of potential love by someone unable to receive it. A gendered analysis highlights the subject's agency, illustrated in the last four lines of the song:

> Now all my love is out
> It's just for you
> It's not a love song
> It's the last song for you

The bulk of Marianne Faithfull's reviews share a tendency to define her as the quintessential survivor. They speak to a deeper issue of men's lack of identification or connection with women that stems from a history written by men who have failed, time and time again, to identify across gender.[8]

Living sober if you were once an addict is a practice. It necessitates a series of repetitions — of acting or reacting the way a normal person would. In AA they say, "fake it 'til you make it," and this is the slogan I have found most applicable in my life. I didn't lose the anxiety, the suicidal ideations, the immobilizing fear that accompanied seemingly mundane daily tasks and chores. I was someone who traveled with Jack Daniels in a soda bottle and brought a flask with me to deposit a check at the bank. I spent most of my life covering up my vulnerability, so when I finally got sober, I was left with a cast of characters, but no distinct sense of self. I am a completely new person. When Marianne got clean, she had to remove thirty-nine years of masks and defense mechanisms. Only when the layers of the onion are effectively peeled back can you start to live, and living sober means navigating a lot of joys, sure, but also disappointment and frustration as a defense mechanism-less open wound. Addicts who no longer drink or do drugs are like living, breathing science experiments. Fucking miracles.

In 2011, Marianne underwent treatment after developing an addiction to sleeping pills—a result of cancer and hepatitis C diagnoses—and was diagnosed with clinical depression. "I was told that I had very likely been clinically depressed for a long, long time, probably since I was 15, or even 14," she said.[9] She spent a week at the Pennsylvania Gestalt Centre and underwent the "open chair" technique: She sat opposite an empty chair and conjured up the decisive moment in her life that had caused the depression and essentially changed history by imagining a positive outcome. She has not felt depressed since.

Marianne's Gestalt depression exorcism occurred after she parted ways with François Ravard in 2009. He was her longest romantic relationship, a man she referred to as her soulmate even though she maintained the position that most relationships were not meant to last. "Mick and I weren't meant to be together forever. With my current lover, it's for life."[10] François did the thing that men so often do, even when they're dating gorgeous, powerful, interesting women—women who deal with health issues, age, and in Marianne's case, get cancer and lose their sex drive—he met someone younger. Marianne didn't even notice until he confessed. Together, they worked out a professional agreement and remain close friends. He stayed on as her manager and even oversaw the production of *Horses and High Heels*, her first album following their separation, which ushered in a new lyrical era in which she dealt with love from the point of view of loss and survival, rather than romance. She overcame a bout of writer's block by writing blunt, confessional lyrics, a trend that continued on the 2014 *Give My Love to London* and the 2018 *Negative Capability*.

Marianne Faithfull has been cheated on. She's been deceived and left for other women. Logically, I know that this happens to everyone, regardless of beauty or status, but it boggles my mind. *Who the fuck leaves Marianne Faithfull?*

Who is more interesting? More beautiful? Show me this mythical woman.

Horses and High Heels is a great break-up album, but it's a great album without having been broken up with, too. It was recorded in New Orleans, released in 2011, and produced by Hal Willner with cameos from Lou Reed, Wayne Kramer of the MC5, and Dr. John. The first single, "Why Did We Have to Part" addresses her separation from Ravard, the overwhelming sense of loss, and the universal problem of letting go. In 2011, I was four years sober and an emotional wreck. In AA, they say you get your marbles back at the five-year mark and, in my personal experience, this is a generous estimate. At the time, I had fallen in lust with a much older woman, an unrequited love affair symptomatic of active addiction. I languished in a state of perpetual craving and listened to Faithfull's rendition of "Stations," co-written by Mark Lanegan and Greg Dulli.

> Oh Mama, ain't no time to fall to pieces
> He has arrived, he has arrived
> There by the Grace of God go I

It's difficult to articulate the despair of addiction, but it's a lot like unrequited love. It triggers the same brain chemicals and renders the host addicted and pathetic. "Stations" is about addiction, even boasting a popular recovery slogan: "There but for the grace of God go I." This adage was originally uttered by evangelical preacher and martyr John

Bradford but was repurposed by Alcoholics Anonymous and makes its way into a song about saving grace during a dark moment. Marianne considered *Horses and High Heels* to be "a very happy record," which seems contradictory. But it's true that by the time it was released, "she wasn't depressed anymore."[11] In true Capricorn fashion, she worked through her heartbreak with an earnest sincerity and created an indelible and lasting document and a new mode of confessional storytelling. An artifact and makeshift portal to the other side.

Situational depression: being in love and left for someone else. It seems masochistic to participate in something that will probably, statistically, not end well. But we search for our counterparts, which, unless you're like a solid puzzle piece — that is, a well-formed person — you're not going to find another piece that fits perfectly. But we roam around smashing ourselves into other puzzle pieces, trying to fit together in a sad, sexy, desperate dance that lasts for a night, a week, a while, maybe forever, but 90 percent of the time ends in disappointment. Insanity: doing this again and again.

Marianne Faithfull's breakthrough with Gestalt therapy happened when she was in her mid-sixties, after a series of health issues, a personal betrayal, and the dissolution of her relationship with François Ravard. I think chronic depression might be a collection of misplaced expectations. Marianne has admitted to marrying when she's bored. She has stopped getting married, and, I think, stopped having sex, but that unfortunate phenomenon has less to do with sex drive and more to do with the organic repercussions of aging. I've looked to women who refuse to compromise their careers, ambitions, ideals because I haven't been able to forfeit mine for more than six months at a time, and it can feel a little lonely when everyone you know is partnered up.

There's also something to be said for relationships that end successfully. Marianne has been married to John Dunbar, Ben Brierly, and Giorgio Della Terza, an American she met at a Narcotics Anonymous meeting—that one did not end well and she does not talk about him. She's also been in long-term, life-changing relationships with men who affected her life in such a way that they were granted lengthy excerpts in her memoirs: Mick Jagger, Oliver Musker, Lord Paddy Rossmore, Howard Tose, and François Ravard. In his 1975 book, *Love and Addiction*, author Stanton Peele argues that the love addict "uses relationships to seal off his inner self from a frightening environment." Like the habitual drug taker, this obsessive quest for companionship distracts from exploring the self and constricts possibility.[12] Romance, however, is culturally sanctioned escapism and a hell of a moneymaker.

Marianne went on a dinner date with Robert Mitchum in 1993. Documentary director Bruce Weber needed Marianne to get personal with Bob, who was characteristically cagey and uncommunicative. They had dinner at Chateau

Marmont and as they exited the restaurant, Mitchum took her in his arms and gave her a classic silver screen kiss. She reflects on being snogged by the last king of Old Hollywood in *Faithfull*:

> I don't know what it would take to get me into bed now. And it's not Catholicism really—it's just too much trouble. The dangers are too great, and the traps are too enormous. Nor am I up for the Mick and Jerry story either: find a partner, settle down and have kids, be respectable, have a normal life. This is much harder for women to do than men.[13]

Most addicts avoid conflict, but being sober entails confrontation and chasing accountability the way we used to chase drugs. Marianne spoke about her relationship with her son, Nicholas Dunbar, in a *Daily Mail* interview in 2007. Nicholas had become a financial analyst and writer who had never done drugs and lived a "quiet, mainstream life."[14] Marianne Faithfull's image is the antithesis of motherhood, and she confessed that she didn't feel like a mother until her son was in his twenties, around the time she grasped sobriety. Before then, he lived with his grandmother and then John Dunbar. Marianne was more of a strung-out apparition, drifting in and out of his life. She describes a heartbreaking scene after the release of *Broken English* when Nicholas flew to New York to spend his vacation with her and Ben. She offered him cocaine when they picked him up from the airport, which he adamantly refused. Their relationship remained fraught until her cancer diagnosis in 2006: "The problem with living life as if there is no tomorrow is that you get to this age and realise that it simply isn't true."[15] A big part of the repairing of that relationship centered on Marianne's failing health and finances. Nicholas offered valuable guidance, imploring her to put away 10 percent of her income, most of which came from touring. At the time of the *Daily Mail* interview, Marianne was sixty years old and had never owned anything—a car, a home, a mortgage. "I've decided to be sensible for the first time ever; to work really, really hard for ten years, and save enough to buy a flat."[16]

Not only did she begin to explore the previously unknown territory of motherhood and economic responsibility in her later years, but she also came to disavow her earlier romanticization of drug-taking. She agrees with nineteenth-century French novelist Gustave Flaubert who suggested that a bourgeois life of adequate sleep, food, and exercise produced the best art.[17] She still considers herself an egomaniac—all addicts are egomaniacs with inferiority complexes—but she is of the mind that habitual drug-taking is a supreme form of narcissism. It's kryptonite for people like her who possess "wilder emotions" and a tendency toward self-sabotage.[18] Her sober life has been quiet and productive while her earlier career was out of control but very newsworthy.

Nine years after *Before the Poison*, *Give My Love to Lon-*

don received similar critical acclaim, boasting the same Nick Cave/Warren Ellis-centric sound and adding collaborations with Roger Waters (again), singer-songwriter Anna Calvi, and Madonna's long-time producer and collaborator Patrick Leonard—and Brian Eno, who stopped by at some point to contribute backing vocals on the Leonard Cohen cover, "Going Home."

By the time she recorded *Give My Love to London* in 2014, she had survived breast cancer, hip surgery, shoulder surgery, a spinal injury, a hepatitis C diagnosis, and the devastating breakup with François. She was sixty-eight years old and single. She considered all of life's big questions in bed with a fractured sacrum:

> I did something that I probably should have done in my 20s. I thought very carefully about who I love, who I don't love, what I care about, what I don't care about, what's important to me, what's not important to me. All the big sorts of things that I had to work out but had never done because I was either parading around in swinging London or I was on drugs—or I was not on drugs but working. I'd never had that sort of absolute peace where I could just ponder on the things that really are important to me and the things that I really don't care about.[19]

The title of the album is a fuck you to the city that created the legend of Marianne Faithfull, the "girl in the rug."

In "Sparrows Will Sing," she pairs the myth with revolutionary imagery — the proletariat 60s waif enacting her revenge on the industry bourgeoisie:

> The young generation is eager to muster the helm
> They cannot be seduced by this candy floss techno-hell
> They put over the hell and the fresh breeze
> They'll sustain
> Calo, calo, cale

The album also boasts deeply personal tracks like "Deep Water," a song co-written by Nick Cave and his young sons.

Her 2018 follow-up, *Negative Capability*, is a continuation of a trend of contemplation, reflection, and appraisal. And this kind of honesty doesn't mean that she's stopped telling stories or inhabiting characters, or wearing masks, as she's described it. There's just less of a need to hide behind the character or the story once you've aged into your own spirit — your ideal self.

"IN MY OWN PARTICULAR WAY"

I do two things, religiously, every winter: I listen to Marianne Faithfull and Google stories about hermits who die in their homes without being discovered for weeks. Years ago, somewhere in Europe, a friendless recluse decomposed into her floor. Her body wasn't discovered until it began dripping into the downstairs neighbor's apartment. Last year, I considered adopting a small dog with a misshapen body and protruding fangs. The disclaimer on the adoption website read, "He did eat his owner." The owner died at home and the dog ate the corpse instead of starving to death, which seems reasonable enough. He has since been adopted and renamed "Rumpelstiltskin."

On November 6, 2018, as I drive to campus for an evening seminar, I play Marianne Faithfull's newest album, *Negative Capability*. I have my period and I feel hormonal and weepy. I rarely cry, and I am confident about my suppression techniques until "In My Own Particular Way" begins and I promptly burst into tears for the first time in a little more than two years. Coincidentally, this also occurs in a campus parking lot. I blame the parking lot, reapply my mascara, and head into class. "In My Own Particular Way" is heartbreaking, but it's not meant to be. In fact, Faithfull insists that this record is about love and that the themes of death, loneliness, and aging are merely a part of that bigger picture.

I don't know why ageism exists in pop culture because women over the age of fifty are inherently more interesting artists and performers. In 2016, Marianne was the subject of a more cerebral version of *MTV Cribs* called *My Place*, and I was pleasantly surprised to find that it was, quite literally, Marianne Faithfull leading an interviewer around her Paris apartment. The episode begins with her asking the camera person not to "fuck about."[1]

"Come on, come on, come on, let's go!"

Marianne's apartment is small and relatively sparse, considering the vast amount of memorabilia and shit she could possess as a well-documented 60s icon. She gestures toward a painting in the living room that states, "the falsehood of truth and the truth of falsehood," and says, "Get a picture of that." In her bedroom, she has about thirty books stacked carefully on one side of a double bed. "I read a lot of books at the same time," she explains. She flips through a few pages. "I like to be on my own." She handles her bedmates with care. The crew follows her out to a small balcony and focuses on her flowers — a makeshift garden that brings her joy. In another scene, she sits in a wooden chair in the middle of her living room, cane in hand, the materialization of the Gypsy Faerie Queen. "I'm pretty lonely actually," she smiles. "That's okay."

I would rather listen to Marianne Faithfull at seventy-four, a woman who sleeps with an assortment of books (and if that's not a mutually beneficial relationship worth striving for, I don't know what is), than be subjected to another trendy twenty-something-year-old cog in the revolving door of streaming music garbage. I would rather be alone forever than lose myself in a relationship. I wonder if that's why Marianne sleeps with books. I would rather be an old, tattered book on Marianne Faithfull's bed, lovingly attended to, than lose myself in a careless person.

Faithfull's personal history is part of her allure and her longevity. It's not often you hear about a hot new geriatric singer. No one is signing new record deals with senior citizens, so the ones who are visible are still adored for a reason. As I mine through live performances on YouTube, I wonder: If I stumbled into a club in New York and saw this woman singing these songs with this band, would I stay? The answer is a resounding yes.

I interviewed Terri Nunn of the band Berlin and confessed that I had seen a number of reunion concerts where the openers were a slew of hip young women wearing mom jeans, playing indistinguishable, guitar-driven indie rock, and that I was forever bored by them. How, once in a great while, someone like Lizzo, Angel Olsen, Cate le Bon, or Amyl and the Sniffers will come along and inject some much-needed substance into pop culture, but I would say 85 percent of contemporary rock music—mainstream or underground—is vapid and uninteresting. Terri thought my new twist on ageism was hilarious. I've been in love with her since I was a child, so it was nice to make my crush of thirty years laugh, but she made an important point: New music isn't about us old farts. Of course, I identify with Liz Phair more than Soccer Mommy, but Soccer Mommy is to young audiences what Liz Phair was to me when I was thirteen. I agree with Terri Nunn. She wrote "Metro," for God's sake. But I'm not sure how to force myself to believe that the majority of new music is substantive enough to stand the test of time. I will always value older women like Marianne, Brenda Lee, or Alice Bag for their roles as pioneers and as mature women who refuse to submit to the pressures of a culture and media that prioritizes youth, sex, and sales over substance.

And yeah, maybe it's because I am aging, but my ageism is *thoughtful*, goddammit. One of my favorite music writers, Jessica Hopper, published a collection of essays a few years ago, and one essay in particular sent me scouring the internet for new music because I refused to be the curmudgeon who fears change and progress—new feminism.[2] She made important points like, of course, earlier feminist music was significant because there was nothing preceding it; that the impact of earlier punk feminism is evident in music today that respects the influence without blatantly ripping it off—which is a good thing; that the struggle of pioneering women has granted them authenticity, but contemporary musicians should not be judged by those same standards; and finally, that struggle and hardship are not necessary ingredients for creating good music.

While I agree with those points, I disagree that just because there are more women making music, that the music they're making is good across the board. I think you can be happy that culture has changed in positive ways — that more girls are playing guitar and starting bands and that more avenues exist in the digital age to support the dissemination of that music to wider audiences. But I think it's disingenuous to argue that more music means more good, meaningful (or feminist) music. And I think it is equally important to identify and disrupt the violence of ageism — this assumption that older women somehow lose the ability to reach new, younger audiences or are bound to history in a way that makes them immutable, unflinching, unchanging. If we, as fans and audiences, should absorb anything, it's how to get old without getting lost.

Our bodies start decomposing, as we live and breathe, pretty early on — like, late twenties, early thirties? I'm not a scientist. "In My Own Particular Way" deals with a subject that is wholly relevant to a significant group of human beings and will someday be immediately relevant to the rest of us. One of these days we might be seventy-four, and some of us might be single, not because there's no one eligible in our Tinder radius, but because we have aged out of romantic love. There's a part of me that feels like I've always been over fifty. My soul is around seventy-two. As I approach forty, solitude becomes less of a choice and more of a social construct. It's harder to make friends as you age. It's harder to score a date at thirty-nine than it is at twenty-five. What Marianne Faithfull conveys in the song is the underlying, sometimes deeply hidden desire to be loved and appreciated, that even the most self-sufficient and stubborn need to thrive. She describes the painful co-nundrum of finally accepting yourself for who you are, but realizing your body has sort of fallen apart in the pro-cess — Benjamin Button in real life.

> Send me someone to love
> Someone who could love me back
> Love me for who I really am
> Not an image and not for money
> I know I'm not young and I'm damaged
> But I'm still pretty, kind and funny
> In my own particular way

There's something sacred about artists who stand the test of time — like they were drawn to become legends through a series of coincidences and divine interventions. And I think this is why we, as fans, are drawn to particular songs and artists and why they sometimes stay with us throughout our lives. Maybe God or the Great Spirit or whatever it is has taken to handpicking Bandcamp pages or social media influencers, but I will always be much more interested in people like the septuagenarian who shot heroin on a wall in Soho and lived to cover "Trouble in Mind" in a way that made me believe she wrote it.

I spent my twenties around musically inclined, self-educated but cultured men. They worshipped punk rock and Tom Waits and introduced me to the films of Jim Jarmusch. When I discovered Alan Rudolph's 1985 film *Trouble in Mind*, I assumed it would grant me admission into their club of niche good taste. *Trouble in Mind* is a neo-film noir fantasy about an ex-cop released from prison into an urban dystopia—well, Seattle—starring Kris Kristofferson, Lori Singer, Keith Carradine, and John Waters's cult hero, Divine, out of drag. Mark Isham wrote and performed the score and recruited Marianne to do vocals. The title track was written by Richard M. Jones in 1926, a blues song that has been interpreted by countless singers and performers.

> Trouble, oh trouble
> Trouble's on your worried mind
> When you see me laughing, baby
> I'm laughing just to keep from crying

Faithfull and Isham's version is an updated, atmospheric take on a classic blues standard, but failed to impress my rock connoisseur housemates. I bought the soundtrack, on vinyl, and kept it to myself.

CAPRICORN

For a practical person, I am very interested in astrology. I was not surprised to learn that Marianne is a Capricorn. She has the symmetrical beauty, stately bearing, heavy eyes, and a dark sense of humor like Marlene Dietrich, who is also a Capricorn. The album *Dreamin' My Dreams* was even stylized, in homage, as a country and western, campy, Dietrich character.[1] Capricorns work hard. They are usually successful but are prone to depression and substance abuse, which might hinder that success. They use their impeccable sense of humor as a mode of deflection. They are fiercely private yet maintain an air of openness and joviality. They are loyal and devoted yet independent and ambivalent when it comes to romantic relationships.

Her ascendant is Taurus, indicating a tendency toward indolence or laziness. Taureans value wealth, stability, comfort, and material things. They are methodical, stubborn, and steadfast, usually with a kind and graceful disposition marred only by the occasional tantrum. Marianne's rising sign expresses itself in her love of fashion and designer clothes. She's been friends with Kate Moss for years and frequented fashion shows with her friend Anita Pallenberg. Her Taurean tendencies also come across in her music, in her preference to slow things down and create lavish soundscapes rather than typical rock anthems.[2]

Marianne Faithfull has a Pisces moon. I've only known a few Pisces in my life, and they were insane, emotional wrecks. According to most astrology websites, Pisces moon people are sensitive, empathetic, affectionate, and prone to idealizing relationships. They can also be melancholic, self-indulgent, evasive, and codependent. Marianne has detailed her ambivalence regarding romantic love and relationships over the years. Having been partnered for most of her life, she admits, interestingly, that her "primal anxiety" is her fear of being consumed by another person.[3] She describes herself as naturally suggestible and easily influenced, which is why she remains self-contained and lives alone. Pisces Moon people are constantly picking up on the feelings of others, along with the mood of the atmosphere around them. This tendency toward uncontrollable emotion and unregulated emotional absorption is the antithesis of the more grounded and pragmatic Capricorn and Taurus. Capricorn especially ain't got time for sentimentality or frivolity. They hold their cards close to their vests and express love through actions rather than words.

According to her chart, Marianne was destined to be a creative spirit, a muse, a junkie, full of love but a complete failure at traditional relationships. I'm not saying that the course of her life was predetermined, but her time, place, and date of birth offers an interesting blueprint upon which lifelong struggles emerge: the conflict between craving wealth and material comforts and desiring to create authentic art; conflicts between love and identity, codependency and freedom; and the struggle to maintain personal autonomy in partnerships.

Marianne has been married three times and partnered a lot for a romantically ambivalent, self-described introvert. John Dunbar, her first husband and the father of her son, lasted one year, but they're still friends and colleagues more than fifty years later. Then there were the four years with that succubus, Mick Jagger. She married punk rocker Ben Brierly and lived in a flat without hot water or electricity during their drug-addled marriage. Her last marriage to Giorgio Della Terza was, in her words, "a nightmare," and he was the only one she didn't like.[4] She was with François for fifteen years. She is of the mind that love is a neurological con job and that falling in love requires an amount of self-deceit that she has been less willing to enact in her more mature years. At the same time, *Negative Capability* is all about love, loneliness, and death. Her perspective on this record, however, extends beyond modern concepts of young, transactional, possessive romantic love — the kind of love pop stars sing about — and reflects a more mature definition and fragile sentimentality. It is a septuagenarian Capricorn woman expressing the contents of her Pisces moon.

I do compatibility charts with famous women regularly. I'm a Gemini sun (with Taurus tendencies), Capricorn rising, and an Aquarius moon. Although Marianne's Pisces moon would put a wrench in the possibility of a sustainable romantic relationship, the earth signs would make for a fruitful friendship. Most of my favorite women are heterosexual, but come off a little gay, including but not limited to all of my romantic interests, one legitimate girlfriend, Judy Garland, Cate Blanchett, and Marianne Faithfull. In this post-binary world, it's easier to see Faithfull's aesthetic, her story, her gender, and genre-bending as inherently queer. We gays are very attracted to struggle — see adopted queer icon Judy Garland, whose funeral may or may not have incited the Stonewall rebellion — and for me, Marianne Faithfull's life, work, and career qualify as struggle, even with the happy ending.

So how does astrology fit into memoiric cultural criticism or into history in general? Does it matter that Marianne Faithfull is a Capricorn and that I have spent an embarrassing amount of time investigating her birth chart and our compatibility? I think the capacity for deep, deep fandom has expanded exponentially in the digital age. Every photo, book, autobiography, interview, anecdote, and astrological breakdown is at our fingertips. Somehow, bits and pieces of rock history once relegated to the bowels of supplemental superficiality — groupie culture, the plaster penises of Cynthia Plaster Caster, teenyboppers — have become worthy of deep insight, and rightfully so. Anything can be a lens through which to examine culture, and the fact that I ever gave a shit whether or not Marianne Faithfull and I were compatible speaks to the personal impact she made on me. The argument goes beyond astrology and extends to the feminization of modes of analysis, like memory, memoir — astrology — and the masculinization of fact, statistics, and quantifiable evidence. What is quantifiable has been recorded and to have your history recorded means that you belong to a group worthy of recording.

So, it is less about astrology and more about the parameters for measuring authenticity. Ninety-nine percent of the reason I decided on graduate school was to legitimize my own work (which I take very seriously, by the way) and to legitimize the lenses through which I observe music and culture. Much of that observation is rooted in archives, research, and documented history. But the other part is more curious, less stringent, and more abstract: it's me in my living room on some freshly downloaded astrology app investigating Marianne Faithfull's planetary placements, our astrological compatibility, and wondering if I, too, will become vulnerable one day.

LOVE IN THE TIME OF CORONAVIRUS

In December 2019, I drafted an email to François Ravard in hopes of securing an interview with Marianne in summer 2020. Now, I am well-versed in meeting, interviewing, and shooting the shit with canonical musical figures, but it had never occurred to me to approach Marianne Faithfull. The first reason being that she doesn't like interviews, and although I'm not a journalist and the interviews I conduct are oral histories and therefore conversational, it is difficult to gain access to musicians who have had bad experiences with the press. The second reason being that, to me, she is like the Mona Lisa of rock 'n' roll, a work of art to be seen from afar but never touched or interacted with. I have interviewed, filmed, and even played music with some of my childhood idols, and most of them are normal people with jobs, families, and no health insurance. Marianne Faithfull exists in another realm, elevated beyond the idols and inhabiting a space reserved for legends. I really can't express just how unfathomable the idea of an interview was. But after sitting on the email draft for a couple of weeks, I sent it to François, who thanked me and suggested we connect in the new year. He told me that he was in Paris and she was living in London. I began preparing to fund-raise for the trip. (I never disclose that I'm broke. It's unprofessional.)

In February, news circulated about a novel coronavirus that had emerged in China. Soon after, Italy was affected, then the United States, and pretty soon the global pandemic had effectively shut down the world. Because our administration is headed by a pathological, narcissistic idiot and his cronies, I was hesitant to believe the gravity of the situation and was mostly concerned with how I would keep working, teaching, and conducting interviews. I mean, my life's work depends on face-to-face interaction, and although I am always thinking about or defending the merits of oral history in relation to more masculine, traditional methodologies, I certainly never thought about the possibility that the in-person interviewing could become obsolete because a virus jumped from a bat to a pangolin to a person who ate a fucking pangolin.

My college classes moved to remote learning, and I had no reason to leave my apartment, which forced me to get back into this manuscript. And then in March, I saw an Instagram post that said Marianne Faithfull had been admitted to the hospital after testing positive for Covid-19. I was devastated. More devastated because she, statistically speaking, was not someone who should recover from this virus. She is technically a senior citizen, a lifelong smoker, and the proud owner of a plethora of other underlying conditions. Marianne remained hospitalized while some of my acquaintances, school associates, friends' parents and grandparents all died, all due to complications from Covid-19. I mourned the Covid-related deaths of John Prine and Marianne's friend and collaborator, Hal Willner, with other friends and fans via social media. I started to feel like a real piece of shit working on this book while some of the people in it were dying at the hands of some invisible grim reaper, and I was not at all sure if the subject of the book would survive. I wondered if I was, after all this time, just a cog in the capitalist wheel. Or was I an addict who needed to work, to have something to strive for in the wake of so much uncertainty?

The most poignant discovery happened right when the news broke, though. I don't think I had ever mourned, really mourned, a celebrity until David Bowie died. I just could not conceive of a life without Bowie in it, and I felt that same pain in my heart when Marianne went to the hospital. I'm not afraid of death, and I know everyone dies, usually alone, but I was not ready to give her up. I couldn't imagine not having her here on earth to look forward to another record in maybe another three or four years. She had survived so much that it seemed cosmically unfair to lose her to a super-virus. If there was an upside to this latest near-death experience, it was the outpouring of love and support that flooded social media. Old people, young people, gays and straights; it seemed like she was everyone's secret lover, and we were connected in our mutual despair at the thought of losing her. A friend of mine said, "Marianne Faithfull has nine lives," but I think it's more like fifty.

Five weeks after being admitted to the ICU, Marianne Faithfull was released from the hospital and returned to her home in London to recuperate.

EPILOGUE: MEMORY, "SHOW ME THE DICK"

What is the legend of Marianne Faithfull? Do women have legends ascribed to them in the same way that Robert Johnson was said to be possessed by the devil and Kurt Cobain lived under that bridge in Aberdeen? Does a woman's rock star, legend-making behavior help or hinder her chances to be remembered?

Whenever people ask me who I'm writing about and I say Marianne Faithfull, the following conversation ensues:

"Sounds so familiar . . ."

"She's a singer."

"Didn't she date the Beatles or something?"

"One of the Rolling Stones."

"RIGHT!"

"But she's also released music for the last fifty years or so."

"So interesting. Mick Jagger . . ."

This inability to locate her begs the question, how do women achieve historical longevity in a culture that doesn't value them or their artistic output? Whose dick do you have to suck to get some respect as an artist? I mean, if not Mick Jagger's, then whose? Show me the dick.

The canon—or men in positions of authority who have constructed a seemingly impenetrable rock dynasty—privileges particular styles of musicianship, virtuosity, and, of course, men. Marianne Faithfull is an artist who has managed to be included in canonical texts and "best of" lists, but who remains largely unrecognizable in popular culture. A new generation of rock music fans can pick Joni Mitchell out of a lineup, but Marianne Faithfull? Not always. Well-known contemporary musicians worship her: Billy Corgan offered to work with her for free after completing *Kissin' Time*, and Warren Ellis tearfully proclaimed his love in a short film documenting the making of *Negative Capability*. She is acknowledged by connoisseurs of rock history, but because she has avoided the trap of nostalgia, she has hardly been noticed in mainstream popular culture, resulting in a lack of recognition among younger generations of rock fans. Her musical output is prolific, and almost consistently well received or heralded by critics, but even when it isn't, there's an underlying respect and veneration beneath tepid reviews. There is no money in iconography and there is no promise of universal recognition. Celebrity is one thing; icon status is another.

Marianne Faithfull walks a fine line between iconography and obsolescence, and it's her own fault. It's hard enough for women to achieve career longevity or historical relevance, but compound that with an eclectic, decades-long career, and the mortal sin of aging, means that the fact that we're still talking about Marianne Faithfull at all is a gender-defying miracle. The Rolling Stones have been patting themselves on the back, touting the same songs, the same live show, the same pelvic thrusts for fifty years, harking back to a time when it meant something. Nostalgia is comfortable, marketable — and most importantly, recognizable. Faithfull escaped from the trap of factory-produced pop stardom and returned to the spotlight as a multifaceted, daring, and experimental artist who refused to subscribe to the tyranny of genre and sentimentality. She continues to expand and explore, without considering why or if it matters, which, I think, is a testament to how much it really does.

Marianne Faithfull is in her seventies and carries a cane now. The cane is, however, more symbolic of legacy than of physical impairment, and she wields it like a scepter, a literal vision of rock royalty. Varying opinions exist on what it means to age gracefully: Women like Madonna are skewered in the press for elevating their asses with implants and flashing their tits, while women who accept their bodies are shunned by the media. Few female performers accept their physical and emotional "deficits" in a way that successfully humanizes them in the eyes of a public bred to demand perfection from its stars. The cane symbolizes Faithfull's progression as a woman and as an artist: from pop star to serious songwriter, from young beauty to elder beauty. There is no right way to age, but hers is pretty close.

Unfortunately for me, Faithfull is unable to tour. I considered seeing her in the early 2000s, but I was completely broke, drunk, and unmotivated. So I'm writing an intimate account about one of the greatest musicians in the history of rock music without having witnessed her mastery beyond the confines of my home. This fact serves a useful, maybe polemical, purpose, though. It dispels the unwritten rule of expert opinion. Like Marianne Faithfull's experience in the rock industry, my experience as a musician, fan, scholar, and historian has been muddled by arbitrary requirements that would quantifiably prove authenticity. Requiring expertise, facts, and expert opinions often means that women rely on male tastemakers, scholars, songwriters, and critics, a habit I hope to dispel by insisting that Faithfull's body of work and my opinions on it have a place in the broader forum of rock historiography.

Faithfull is not a household name anymore, but she should be. Well, she's not a household name to a new generation of music listeners, but she is still enthusiastically remembered as the singer/waif/style icon to superfans who grew up with her and are now in their sixties and seventies, as well as to young connoisseurs and music nerds. People, myself included, throw the word "icon" around like it means something. While being an icon, or iconic, implies a sense of respect and reverence, it eludes celebrity or mass appeal. As a matter of fact, some great icons are idolized by small factions of music fans in niche corners and subsets of larger rock culture and die in esoteric, respectable obscurity. Faithfull has had the privilege of experiencing celebrity and chose to eschew mainstream stardom in favor of remaining authentic, and though the two are not mutually exclusive, more often than not, they are. She chose to determine her own narrative, make her own choices once she returned to the industry, and exert her autonomy as both a woman and an artist—decisions that aren't exactly synonymous with making shitloads of money. I don't see much use in the word "icon" unless it can be weaponized and used to pry open the gates of mainstream media and insist that someone like Marianne Faithfull is worth talking about, or unless it's a word that turns into dollar bills and can be used to financially support a woman who has done so much for women in rock and popular culture. Representation matters.

I interviewed Cindy Wilson of the B-52s a few years ago in a hotel room in Manhattan. I asked how she felt about their Rock & Roll Hall of Fame absence—it was around the time that nominees had been announced—and she said "Oh, we don't care about that. It's corporate crap," which I thought was a perfect answer from one of the most anti-establishment, inventive bands on the face of the planet. It wasn't until weeks later, when I had finished editing the interview, that I considered how much the Hall of Fame does matter for the very same reason I asked her about it. Mainstream popular culture is how the majority of the public gets their news or, in this case, how they absorb musical knowledge. A B-52s induction would introduce a new generation of fans to the influential work of a seminal new wave band.

Out of the 330 musicians and bands inducted into the Rock & Roll Hall of Fame, only forty-seven are women. Marianne Faithfull has been eligible since 1989, the year the Rolling Stones were inducted, but she has never been nominated. Stevie Nicks is the first (and only) woman to be inducted twice. Dusty Springfield and Joan Baez, Marianne's female peers, have both been inducted, and they are more likely to be identified in a lineup of "women in rock." I wanted to write a popular, accessible book about Marianne Faithfull because she has done so much for me personally with the music she's made and because I genuinely care that people know how instrumental she was to rock culture — how important she continues to be. I have an affinity for women who have survived addiction and other obstacles (self-imposed or not), and Marianne Faithfull is someone whose history, work, and legacy are overshadowed by her past and especially by her affiliations with certain rock star men. Her objective legacy is her role in the British Invasion — as one of the first successful female artists and a woman who, for better or worse, ushered in a new era of celebrity culture — but most importantly, her legacy is her prolificacy and the range and diversity of her musical output for more than fifty years. It is almost unheard of for an artist to maintain their credibility in the music industry for that long.

I have very little faith in media gatekeepers and those at

the helm of institutions like the Hall of Fame. I do, how-ever, have faith in people and in their capacity to remain curious and to insist on gender parity within those insti-tutions. I hope that I've made you curious about Marianne Faithfull, and that you talk about her, and that the conver-sation continues forever.

ACKNOWLEDGMENTS

"Marianne Faithfull: Diary of a Lesbian Spinster in Winter" is the essay that birthed *Why Marianne Faithfull Matters*. It was published by *Memoir Mixtapes*, a totally unique music blog run by Samantha Lamph and Kevin Woodall, in winter 2019. Gianna LaMorte, one of my biggest cheerleaders and admirer of The Women of Rock Oral History Project, read the essay and sent me a message that she will regret for the rest of her life:

"When are you going to turn this into a book?"

She connected me to Casey Kittrell who encouraged me through the submission process, and the rest is history. I would like to thank Gianna, Casey, Evelyn McDonnell, and Jessica Hopper at the University of Texas Press for creating space for accessible music scholarship—and for indulging more, er, unique forms of expression. This book was a pleasure to write. Special thanks to Sally Furgeson for making it readable.

To Marianne Faithfull, I hope you do not find this book scaly and that it reads more as the love letter I intended. Thank you for living and for continuing to produce meaningful work. I am so glad I get to exist in this life with you.

My real relationship with Marianne Faithfull began well into my sobriety, and in many ways this book marks my coming of age, later in life, with a woman who came of age, later in life. Her work offered me a blueprint with which to navigate the shit storm that is sobriety, full of heartbreak and disappointment, but also joy and friendship. Everything I have accomplished since August 1, 2007, I have accomplished because I am sober. I owe all my thanks to my recovery family — you know who you are.

The Smith College Ada Comstock Scholars Program changed my life and transformed me into the confident, insufferable woman I am today. I would not have made the transition without Sid Dalby, Erika Laquer, Debra Carney, Shelly Cotnoir, and Karen Sise, who helped me navigate my overwhelming new life. Thank you to my undergrad advisers, Susan Van Dyne, Kelly Anderson, and Steve Waksman (the Dr. of Rock) for their invaluable and continued support. To the Sophia Smith Collection/Smith College Special Collections for housing the Women of Rock Oral History Project. It has literally given me a life and a purpose — and got me into grad school.

Thank you to the University of Massachusetts (graduate history department and press) Mary Lashway, Chris Appy, Jennifer Fronc, Joel Wolfe, and Matt Becker.

I spend a lot of time alone because, as I expressed in the book, I am a true introvert, but there are some people who may have tired of hearing about Marianne Faithfull, listening to Marianne Faithfull, reading this manuscript, or hearing me talk about this book: Courtney Naliboff and Alex Fullerton, thank you. Sean Donovan, Crystal Ford, Chad Lazarri, Mac McDonald, Mills Taylor, Willow Fortin,

Acknowledgments

Debbie Richards, Sophia Cacciola, Michael J. Epstein, Jason and Pam Layne, Sarissa Markowitz, Brad Logan, Jen Dessinger, and Piper Preston. To my family and niece and nephew, Everly and Hudson, who will not be allowed to read this until they're thirty, Carolyn Innes, Meryl Fingrutd, Jenna Swotchak, and my dog, Andrew.

Gratitude is a new thing for me—not because I am inherently ungrateful, but because my baseline is sort of neurotic impatience and mild disappointment. As soon as I'm finished with something, I move on to the next thing to avoid an existential crisis. Reflection seems too dangerous! Honestly, I looked at the back of other books to see if I had left anything important out. "Ah, the acknowledgments." Typical.

DISCOGRAPHY AND FILMOGRAPHY

Albums

Marianne Faithfull, 1965
Come My Way, 1965
Go Away from My World, 1965
North Country Maid, 1966
Love in a Mist, 1967
Dreamin' My Dreams, 1976[1]
Broken English, 1979
Dangerous Acquaintances, 1981
A Child's Adventure, 1983
Rich Kid Blues, 1985[2]
Strange Weather, 1987
Blazing Away, 1990 (live)
A Secret Life, 1995
20th Century Blues, 1997
The Seven Deadly Sins, 1998
Vagabond Ways, 1999
Kissin' Time, 2002
Before the Poison, 2005
Live at the BBC, 2008
Easy Come, Easy Go, 2008
Horses and High Heels, 2011
Give My Love to London, 2014
Negative Capability, 2018

Compilation Albums

The World of Marianne Faithfull, 1969
As Tears Go By, 1981
Summer Nights, 1984

Discography and Filmography

Marianne Faithfull, 1984
Faithfull — A Collection of Her Best Recordings, 1994
Best of Marianne Faithfull, 1998
A Perfect Stranger: The Island Anthology, 1998
A Stranger on Earth — An Introduction to Marianne Faithfull, 2001
The Collection, 2005

Singles

As Tears Go By/Greensleeves, 1964
Blowin' in the Wind/House of the Rising Sun, 1964
Come and Stay With Me/What Have I Done Wrong, 1965
This Little Bird/Morning Sun, 1965
Summer Nights/The Sha La La Song, 1965
Yesterday/Oh Look Around You, 1965
Tomorrow's Calling/That's Right Baby, 1966
Counting/I'd Like to Dial Your Number, 1966
Is This What I Get for Loving You?/Tomorrow's Calling, 1967
Something Better/Sister Morphine, 1969
Dreamin' My Dreams/Lady Madeleine, 1975
All I Want to Do in Life/Wrong Road Again, 1976
The Way You Want Me to Be/That Was the Day, 1978
The Ballad of Lucy Jordan/Brain Drain, 1979
Broken English/What's the Hurry, 1980
Broken English/Why D'Ya Do It, 1980
Intrigue/For Beauty's Sake, 1981
Sweetheart/Over Here, 1982
Broken English/Sister Morphine, 1982
Running for Our Lives/She's Got a Problem, 1983
As Tears Go By/Trouble in Mind, 1987
Don't Forget Me/20th Century Blues/Mack the Knife, 1996
Hang It on Your Heart, 1997
Vagabond Ways/Electra/For Wanting You/Wilder Shores of Love, 1999
Electra, 1999
Sex with Strangers, 2002

Easy Come, Easy Go, 2004
Horses and High Heels, 2011

Feature Films

Made in the U.S.A., 1966
I'll Never Forget What's 'isname, 1967
The Girl on a Motorcycle, 1968
Lucifer Rising, 1972
Ghost Story, 1974
Assault on Agathon, 1976
When Pigs Fly, 1993
Shopping, 1994
Moondance, 1995
Crimetime, 1996
Intimacy, 2001
Far from China, 2001
Nord-Plage, 2004
Paris, je t'aime, 2006
Marie Antoinette, 2006
Irina Palm, 2007
Faces in the Crowd, 2011
Belle du Seigneur, 2012

1. Repackaged and re-released in 1978 as *Faithless*.
2. *Rich Kid Blues* was first recorded in 1971.

NOTES

Introduction

1. Marianne Faithfull and David Dalton, *Faithfull: An Autobiography* (New York: Cooper Square Press, 2000), 293.

Parents

1. Mark Hodkinson, *Marianne Faithfull: As Years Go By* (London: Omnibus Press, 2013), 9.
2. Marianne Faithfull and David Dalton, *Faithfull: An Autobiography* (New York: Cooper Square Press, 2000), 4.
3. Hodkinson, *Marianne Faithfull*, 7.
4. Ibid., 8.
5. Faithfull's maternal grandmother was Jewish.
6. Hodkinson, *Marianne Faithfull*, vii.
7. Ibid.
8. Marianne Faithfull and François Ravard, *Marianne Faithfull: A Life on Record* (New York: Rizzoli, 2014).
9. "Marianne Faithfull: Keeping the Faith," *Close Up*, BBC, April 27, 2009, bbc.co.uk/programmes/b0077vhw.
10. What Rolling Stones manager Andrew Loog Oldham allegedly exclaimed the first time he saw Marianne Faithfull.
11. Faithfull and Dalton, *Faithfull*, 14.
12. Hodkinson, *Marianne Faithfull*, 289.
13. Ibid., 15.
14. Ibid., 15–16.
15. Faithfull and Dalton, *Faithfull*, 20.
16. Marianne is the only child of Eva and Glynn Faithfull. She has an adopted brother, Chris O'Dell, and half-siblings from Glynn's second marriage.

Notes

The British Invasion

1. Craig Morrison, "The British Invasion at 50: A Musical Phenomenon," *Concordia University News*, January 30, 2014, concordia.ca/cunews/main /stories/2014/01/30/the-british-invasionat50amusicalphenomenon.html.

2. "The Rolling Stones Introduce Bluesman Howlin' Wolf on US TV, One of the 'Greatest Cultural Moments of the 20th Century' (1965)," *Open Culture*, August 8, 2016, openculture.com/2016/08/the-rolling-stones -introduce-bluesman-howlin-wolf-on-us-tv.html.

3. Genya Ravan, interview by Tanya Pearson, Women of Rock Oral History Project, January 2018.

4. Marianne Faithfull and David Dalton, *Faithfull: An Autobiography* (New York: Cooper Square Press, 2000), 21.

5. Faithfull and Dalton, *Faithfull*, 42–43.

6. Joan W. Scott, "Gender: A Useful Category of Historical Analysis," *American Historical Review* 91, no. 5 (December 1986).

7. Sheila Whitely and Jennifer Rycenga, *Queering the Popular Pitch* (New York: Routledge, 2006), xiii, quoted in Jodie Taylor, *Playing It Queer: Popular Music, Identity and Queer World-Making* (New York: Peter Lang, 2010), 3.

8. "Marianne Faithfull—Interview + Song for Nico," *Dialogues*, September 1, 2015, youtube.com/watch?v=asLU-brhDJQ.

Pop Stardom

1. For example, the members of the 27 Club—including Jim Morrison, Jimi Hendrix, Brian Jones, and Janis Joplin—all died at twenty-seven.

2. Mark Hodkinson, *Marianne Faithfull: As Years Go By* (London: Omnibus, 2013), 32.

3. Ibid., 33.

4. Ibid., 34.

5. "Marianne Faithfull: Keeping the Faith," *Close Up*, BBC, April 27, 2009, bbc.co.uk/programmes/b0077vhw.

6. Peter Jones, "Marianne Faithfull Is a 'Real' Nice Person," *Record Mirror*, August 1964.

7. Hodkinson, *Marianne Faithfull*, 43.
8. Ibid.
9. The title of a 1966 song by British band, the Kinks.
10. Hodkinson, *Marianne Faithfull*, 52.
11. Marianne Faithfull and David Dalton, *Faithfull: An Autobiography* (New York: Cooper Square Press, 2000), 14.
12. Ibid., 79.
13. Ibid., 162.

Breasts

1. Tammy Hughes, "Time Has Not Treated Her Well . . . Former Sixties Siren Marianne Faithfull Is Unrecognizable," *Daily Mail*, June 15, 2012, dailymail.co.uk/tvshowbiz/article-2159808/Shocking-images-reveal -time-took-toll-swinging-sixties-sweetheart-Marianne-Faithfull.html.
2. The iconic black leather jumpsuit she wore in the film *The Girl on a Motorcycle* in 1968.
3. "Technophallus" is a term coined by my friend, adviser, and professor of rock and popular culture, Dr. Steve Waksman.

"Wild Horses Couldn't Drag Me Away"

1. Mark Hodkinson, *Marianne Faithfull: As Years Go By* (London: Omnibus, 2013), 93.
2. Ibid., 115.
3. Marianne Faithfull and David Dalton, *Faithfull: An Autobiography* (New York: Cooper Square Press, 2000), 113.
4. Hodkinson, *Marianne Faithfull*, 143.
5. Ibid.
6. "Marianne Faithfull: Keeping the Faith," *Close Up*, BBC, April 27, 2009, bbc.co.uk/programmes/b0077vhw.
7. *Marianne Faithfull: Live in Hollywood*, recorded spring 2005, DVD.
8. Faithfull and Dalton, *Faithfull*, 204.
9. Ibid., 214.
10. Ibid., 212.

Notes

11. Simon Hattenstone, "Kenneth Anger: 'No, I Am Not a Satanist,'" *Guardian*, March 10, 2010, theguardian.com/film/2010/mar/10/kenneth-anger-interview.

Trauma Is a Gateway Drug

1. John Walsh, "Marianne Faithfull: I Was Saved by Sex," *Independent*, February 28, 2002.
2. I still do not smoke and it's not Marianne Faithfull's fault that I was an impressionable and insecure teen who didn't hit puberty until my senior year of high school.
3. Marianne Faithfull and David Dalton, *Memories, Dreams and Reflections* (London: Harper Perennial, 2008), 99.
4. Marianne Faithfull and David Dalton, *Faithfull: An Autobiography* (New York: Cooper Square Press, 2000), 221.
5. Mark Hodkinson, *Marianne Faithfull: As Years Go By* (London: Omnibus, 2013), 198.
6. Ibid., 231.

A Punk Comeback

1. Punk is often condensed into Ramones and Clash biopics, oral histories of East and West Coast US punk, and histories of UK punk that ignore the integral roles played by women. Bands and artists like the Slits, the B Girls, and Alice Bag are reclaiming their place in the annals of 70s punk history by taking charge of their own narratives.
2. Betty Friedan, *The Feminine Mystique* (New York: W. W. Norton, 1963).
3. It didn't.

Strange Weather

1. Line from Elton John's 1973 "Candle in the Wind."
2. Marianne Faithfull and David Dalton, *Faithfull: An Autobiography* (New York: Cooper Square Press, 2000), 273.
3. Ibid., 278.

4. Ibid.

5. Chris Morris, "Marianne Faithful — Strange Weather," *Chicago Reader*, January 3, 2020, chicagoreader.com/chicago/marianne-faithful — strange -weather/Content?oid=871810.

6. Edward Rothstein, "Faithfull Discovers a Rocker Within Weill," *New York Times*, April 11, 1995.

The '90s

1. Steven Hyden, "The Legacy of Woodstock '99 Is Sexual Assault," *Ringer*, August 13, 2019, theringer.com/2019/8/13/20801339/break-stuff-episode -six-sexual-assaults-woodstock-99.

2. The festival was revived once in 2010. Marsha Lederman, "Sarah McLachlan Says Lilith Fair Is Over," *Globe and Mail*, March 8, 2011, theglobeandmail.com/arts/music/sarah-mclachlan-says-lilith-fair -is-over/article569791.

3. Susan Faludi, *The Terror Dream: Fear and Fantasy in Post-9/11 America* (New York: Scribe, 2008).

4. Marianne Faithfull and David Dalton, *Faithfull: An Autobiography* (New York: Cooper Square Press, 2000), 295.

5. *Live in Hollywood* was recorded in 2005. "Times Square" was performed with Barry Reynolds, but the song also appears on her 1983 studio album *A Child's Adventure*.

Before the Poison

1. Marianne Faithfull and David Dalton, *Memories, Dreams and Reflections* (London: Harper Perennial, 2008), 216.

2. Kembrew McLeod, "A Critique of Rock Criticism in North America," *Popular Music* 20, no. 1 (2001): 47.

3. Peter Jones, "Marianne Faithfull Is a 'Real' Nice Person," *Record Mirror*, August 1964.

4. "Nude Girl in a Rug at Stones Party," *Evening Times*, June 28, 1967.

5. "Marianne Faithfull: Reinventing a Rock Legend," interview by Rita Houston, *Favorite Sessions*, NPR, September 8, 2011.

6. Mark Millan, review of *A Child's Adventure*, *Daily Vault*, September 14, 2009.

7. Stephen Deusner, "Marianne Faithfull: Before the Poison," *Pitchfork*, January 23, 2005, pitchfork.com/reviews/albums/2962-before-the -poison.

8. Robert Palmer, *Rock & Roll: An Unruly History* (New York: Harmony Books, 1995), 249.

9. Mark Hodkinson, *Marianne Faithfull: As Years Go By* (London: Omnibus, 2013), 343.

10. Ibid., 329.

11. Alex Ramon, "Marianne Faithfull: Horses and High Heels," *Pop Matters*, May 19, 2011, popmatters.com/139631-marianne-faithfull-horses-and -high-heels-2496049506.html.

12. Stanton Peele and Archie Brodsky, *Love and Addiction* (New York: Taplinger Publishing, 1975), 98.

13. Marianne Faithfull and David Dalton, *Faithfull: An Autobiography* (New York: Cooper Square Press, 2000), 290.

14. Jenny Johnston, "The Life, Loves, and Hell of Marianne Faithfull," *Daily Mail*, April 8, 2007, dailymail.co.uk/femail/article-447189/The-life-loves -hell-Marianne-Faithfull.html.

15. Ibid.

16. Ibid.

17. Hodkinson, *Marianne Faithfull*, 337.

18. Ibid., 336.

19. Kory Grow, "50 Years of Tears: Marianne Faithfull's Amazing Second Act," *Rolling Stone*, November 25, 2014, rollingstone.com/music/music-news /50-years-of-tears-marianne-faithfulls-amazing-second-act-41274.

"In My Own Particular Way"

1. "My Place: Marianne Faithfull," *Nowness: Culture in Motion*, October 19, 2016, youtube.com/watch?v=2MhwlTwLHx4&t=27s.

2. Jessica Hopper, *The First Collection of Criticism by a Living Female Rock Critic* (Chicago: Featherproof Books, 2015).

Capricorn

1. Marianne Faithfull and David Dalton, *Faithfull: An Autobiography* (New York: Cooper Square Press, 2000), 224.
2. Ibid.
3. Ibid., 47.
4. Alison Jane Reid, "Marianne Faithfull: A Modern Helen of Troy," *Ethical Hedonist Magazine*, March 8, 2011.

Why Solange Matters

by Stephanie Phillips

Growing up in the shadow of her superstar sister, Beyoncé, and defying an industry that attempted to bend her to its rigid image of a Black woman, Solange Knowles has become a pivotal musician and artist in her own right.

In *Why Solange Matters*, Stephanie Phillips chronicles the creative journey of Solange, a beloved voice of the Black Lives Matter generation. A Black feminist punk musician herself, Phillips addresses not only the unpredictable trajectory of Solange's career but also how she and other Black women see themselves through the musician's repertoire. First, she traces Solange's progress through an inflexible industry, charting the artist's development up to 2016, when the release of her third album, *A Seat at the Table*, redefined her career. With this record and then *When I Get Home* (2019), Phillips describes how Solange has embraced activism, anger, Black womanhood and intergenerational trauma to inform her remarkable art.

Why Solange Matters not only cements the subject in the pantheon of world-changing twenty-first-century musicians, it introduces its writer as an important new voice.

'A significant and sober treatise on popular music . . . This book is more than necessary.' Thurston Moore

faber

'Phillips presses our ear to the street in order to reveal how Solange broke the mould and released us all.' Shana L. Redmond, author of *Everything Man: The Form and Function of Paul Robeson*

'Phillips's study of female self-empowerment and cultivating racial identity in all-white spaces gives readers a much-needed look into staying true to yourself within a challenging music industry.' Laina Dawes, author of *What Are You Doing Here?: A Black Woman's Life and Liberation in Heavy Metal*

'The author's prose sparkles . . . This is a book about what freedom could look like for Black women.' Caleb Azumah Nelson, *Observer*

Why Karen Carpenter Matters

by Karen Tongson

A *Pitchfork* Music Book of the Year, 2019
Nominated for a Lambda Literary Award in
LGBTQ+ Non-Fiction, 2020

In the 1960s and 1970s, America's music scene was marked by raucous excess, reflected in the tragic overdoses of young superstars such as Jimi Hendrix and Janis Joplin. At the same time, the uplifting harmonies and sunny lyrics that propelled Karen Carpenter and her brother, Richard, to international fame belied a different sort of tragedy – the underconsumption that led to Karen's death at age thirty-two from the effects of an eating disorder.

In *Why Karen Carpenter Matters*, Karen Tongson (whose parents named her after the pop icon) interweaves the story of the singer's rise to fame with her own trans-Pacific journey between the Philippines – where imitations of American pop styles flourished – and Karen Carpenter's home ground of Southern California. Tongson reveals why the Carpenters' chart-topping, seemingly white-washed musical fantasies of 'normal love' have profound significance for her – as well as for other people of colour, LGBTQ+ communities, and anyone outside the mainstream culture usually associated with Karen Carpenter's legacy.

faber

A radical, literary and intimate insight into one of the twentieth century's most vital artists, this hybrid of memoir and biography excavates the destructive perfectionism at the root of the Carpenters' sound, while finding the beauty in the singer's all-too-brief life.

'Tongson serves up a number of astute observations about fantasy, projection, longing, normalcy, and aberrance.' Maggie Nelson, author of *The Argonauts*

'[Tongson] deftly weaves memoir, history, and cultural criticism to highlight the dynamic relationship between artists and listeners.' *Pitchfork*, Best Music Books of 2019

'Engrossing . . . An enthusiastic and persuasive Carpenters fan, Tongson is also a stellar critic with extensive knowledge of music and songcraft . . . a triumphant delight.' *4Columns*